ShagMail.com presents...

The Best of
Bizarre News II

UNCENSORED!

D0110562

Spanning The Globe For The
Weird...Strange...and Stupid

www.bizarrenews.com

For my readers who make Bizarre
worth writing. - Lewis

* * * Table of Contents * * *

A note from Bizarre News Editor, Lewis

Greetings Fellow Bizarros:

Well, here it is…The Best of Bizarre II. I am wondering if we can create a ShagMail version of Rocky. This book goes where the first edition feared to tread. We have included stories that simply could not make it into our twice a week publication. In other words, it was deemed too hot or controversial to include in the email version. The one thing that is certain: there is plenty of bizarreness in the world and we are just scratching the surface. The Best of Bizarre News II tries to get beneath the surface.

A lot has happened since we first took over Bizarre News. For those who may not know, we purchased Bizarre News and changed the format way back in April of 1999. I was not a full-time employee of ShagMail at the time, mostly substituting for TZ at Laff A Day. But then Bizarre News started to take off and I was hired full time. Radio stations across the country routinely use our stories. Magazines all over the world use our stuff. Everyone seems to want a piece of Bizarre News. And as our subscribership grew, we have added a lot of help. We now have three people contributing stories and several readers who have become "stringers" for us.

But Bizarre News works first and foremost because of you readers. Your contribution to this creative endeavor is unlike any publication in the ShagMail family. We now have over 600,000 subscribers that receive Bizarre News twice a week. Some of you even read it.

Let's see, what has happened since the last book? My son has come of age and occasionally submits a story or two…and a column here and there. I am training him in what qualifies as bizarre. After doing this for so long, you kind of get jaded as to what is weird enough to share.

The danger is that we begin to push the envelope further and further. But when you start as far out as we did, one can only hope that we stop short of moving too far.

When folks ask me what I do for a living, I am not sure what to tell them. Am I an investigative journalist? Well, sort of, since what Bizarre News does try to do is investigate stories that you will not get to read about in your local paper. Investigating the Florida Skunk Ape in is not something the New York Times dares to cover.

Reviewing past stories and picking out the best (as well as those that were too hot for general consumption) has been a riot. We have four people rummaging through the material. How do you choose? There was the time I interviewed the Porn Queen, Candice…should this have made the cut? How about my harrowing visit to Israel and Gaza? Little did I know then that the problems would get worse and are still raging.

One of my favorite pastimes is to see what exactly the boss will approve for my expenses. When I suggested that he allow me to put 900 number charges on the company tab, it was almost as good as him springing for a brothel visit. While we did manage to get a story or two from it, the accountant wasn't too pleased with the $876 charge. I am thorough if I am nothing else.

All in all, this book is better than the first. It is longer and packed with more of the stuff you want to read. A special thanks to Allison, Gail, Jane and yes, our chief editor Joe. He actually made it on the Sally Jesse Raphael show to promote the first book. Bizarre News is a collaborative affair and we are still trying to turn this thing into a television show. Stay tuned and thanks for reading.

Lewis

1

On the Trail of the Bizarre

Pursuit of the bizarre leads down many paths. Whether it's everyday people committing unbelievable acts of stupidity, artists pushing the extremes of poor taste or social criminals inventing outrageous new sexual fetishes, the different varieties of bizarre always manage to shock, amaze and frequently disgust. In this chapter we will take an uncompromising look at a broad cross-section of bizarreness from Pasadena to Pakistan covering everything from sex slaves to kinky poltergeists. Consider this chapter your bizarre primer.

Snout to Bring Sweet Smell of Success?

TAIWAN - In order to acquire a little good luck this year, a Taiwanese man asked a cosmetic surgeon to change his nose into the shape of a pig's snout. The man's pig-nose wish is one of scores of unusual requests received by surgeons in the run up to the New Year, with Chinese people aiming to improve their luck as the country's economy takes a turn for the worse. According to traditional Chinese beliefs, the shape of a person's face determines the extent of their good luck and fortune, and in Chinese society pigs are regarded as a symbol of wealth and a comfortable life. However, this man's good fortune obviously hasn't kicked in yet because the cosmetic surgeon told him to find another doctor willing to carry out the bizarre request.

Penis Ice Sculpture Gets a Rise Out of Residents

COLUMBIA, Connecticut - A six-foot snow and ice sculpture depicting a penis got a rise out of residents in the town of Columbia, Connecticut. Police have been asked to destroy the erected sculpture and one politician stated she would have knocked it over herself but it was bigger than her. A shocked worker at a nearby nursery school told reporters, "It was so perfect. It was like artwork. It was so real."

Sex Service Tells Golfers What to Do with Their Balls

PASADENA, California - Callers wishing to hear information about an upcoming U.S. amateur golf tournament heard about more than their golf balls. A one-digit error published in 100,000 brochures for the Tournament of Roses in Pasadena, California, led callers to a sex line instead of the golf line. Caryn Eaves Person, the event's spokeswoman, told reporters, "As everyone knows who works with printed materials, mistakes happen."

Lush Looks For Lizard Love on Livingston

ORLANDO, Florida - A drunken man in Orlando must have had his beer goggles on too tight when he stumbled out of the Eight Seconds bar on Livingston Street and attacked a five-foot lizard statue. The amorous embrace snapped the statue from its base which in turn sent both the drinker and the lizard crashing to the ground. The city reportedly has 60 of these huge lizard statues on its streets as part of an arts project and are said to cost approximately $3,800 a piece. Sergeant Scott Boos described the man as being "a little drunk" and was perhaps looking for "a little lizard love." No charges have been made against the man; however, city authorities may seek money to repair the statue.

Artist Licks Gender Discrimination With Jelly Boobs

EAST LONDON - Artist Sally Barker is trying to lick gender discrimination by exhibiting jelly sculptures of her friends' breasts. A total of six pairs of breasts, ranging from a size 32A to a 38DD, are to be shown at East London's Institute of Contemporary Art, and come in orange, lime, strawberry, raspberry, lemon and blackcurrant flavors. Barker, 38, has titled the work "Jelly Tits" because she claimed she was bored of using traditional bronze or stone. Gallery boss Matthew Higgs described Barker's display as being "a simple and playful theme which shows how women continue to be objectified for how they look rather than what they do."

What Are We Going To Do For Bizarre Laws Now?

ARIZONA - Arizona plans to pass a bill to repeal archaic sex laws. The legislation repeals century-old laws that forbid unmarried cohabitation, sodomy, and sex that is not intended to conceive children. Governor Jane Hull has not yet decided if she will sign the bill. If she decides to veto it, the bill must go back to the state legislature.

Demo Crew Brings Wrong House Down

TEXARKANA, Arkansas - "Oops" followed by a few other choice words were probably the expressions used by a demolition crew after realizing they accidentally knocked down the wrong house. Johnny Mack Richardson, of Richardson Environmental and Excavating Services in Texarkana, Arkansas, told reporters that they had been sitting on the street when they made a call to City Hall asking if they had the right house. "They asked us if there were trees covering it up, and we said yes. They said: "Then you're at the right place." Richard concluded by saying, "Evidently there were two houses that were covered by trees."

Hungry Party-goer Gets Burned By Frozen Pastry

VIENNA - A hungry party-goer in Austria got in trouble with the Heat when he decided to defrost a frozen doughnut with a candle. The 19-year-old fire starter evidentially was not satisfied with the snacks provided at the party he was attending at the Ferstl Palace in Vienna, so he began rummaging through the kitchen. Upon finding a doughnut in the freezer and apparently with no microwave in sight, he brought the pastry into the living room to defrost it with a candle. However, in the process he ignited a sofa and the blaze quickly spread to wood paneling. Some 600 guests were evacuated from the building without incident. However, the young man was injured as he tried unsuccessfully to extinguish the blaze before it could spread further.

Shriners and Nude Dancers - Perfect Combo

WINNIPEG, Manitoba - A group of Shriners has sparked a major uproar in Winnipeg after it was reported the fez-festooned members held a men-only fundraiser for sick children that featured nude dancers and public sex acts. The controversy erupted following newspaper reports that a "Gentlemen's Dinner" fundraiser, organized by the Shriners' motor patrol unit, included two nude dancers who climbed on top of a banquet table where several men touched and engaged in oral sex with them in front of hundreds of male guests.

Breast Milk Keeps Stranded Boating Victims Afloat

PUERTO RICO - A group of stranded boating victims made the breast of a bad situation. Young mother Elena Mercedes managed to keep the crew afloat, so to speak, when they ran out of food by having each person suckle milk from her breasts. Each sucked Mercedes's breasts for just a few seconds a day, while she was fed by mouth by her sister. The group made the journey in the hope of finding work in Puerto Rico, but their wooden boat's compass broke and they drifted back to shore after 12 days. All passengers are said to be doing fine, although Mercedes apparently hasn't been able to breastfeed since the ordeal.

Plan For First Nude Medical Clinic Dies On Table

NAPLES, Florida - *The St. Petersburg Times* reported that Dr. William Charles Leach has been given an indefinite suspension by the Florida Board of Medicine for exposing himself to his patients. On at least three separate occasions Dr. Leach has dropped his pants, discussed medical charts in the buff, and attempted to conduct examinations in various stages of undress. "...he took off his laboratory coat and his shirt and pants," commented one patient. "He then stood naked in front of [me] and asked me to comment on his appearance." Leach has stated that he plans to create the first nude medical clinic in Florida, but complaints by patients have prompted the board to suspend him, aborting the project prematurely.

Atheist Tries to Sell His Soul on eBay

Here is further proof that people will try to sell anything on the Internet. Adam Burtle from Seattle put his soul up for auction on the trading website eBay. The 20-year-old received bids ranging from $6.66 from an ex-girlfriend to a top bid of $400. The sale listing has since been removed from the site, because according to eBay spokesman Kevin Pursglove, "You have to have a piece of merchandise that a seller can deliver to a buyer." Items previously put up for auction include organs, drugs and even a person's virginity.

Japanese Hard on Chinese Viagra Contraband

TOKYO, Japan - A soft drink containing the active ingredient of the impotence drug Viagra has been banned by Japanese officials. Some 47,000 bottles of the non-prescription drink were imported from China last year, and all but 4,000 have already been sold. Each bottle of the drink contained 64.3 milligrams of the chemical sildenafil, far more than the 25 or 50 mg in one tablet of Viagra sold in Japan, officials said. The ban was put into effect shortly after advertisements for the drink, touted as "the solution to your nighttime problems," appeared in men's magazines and on the Internet...obviously hoping to tap into the market of an estimated 9.8 million men in Japan who suffer from erectile dysfunction.

Internet Group Lends Support to the Well Endowed

There is a new website being established to lend support to men with large penises. The website says it caters to those men with large penises and those who have been injured by one. The site's home page reassures everyone, "While it is true that 1.5% of home accidents are caused by large penis-related incidents, only a small number have ever been known to be fatal."

A New Kind of San Francisco Treat?

SAN FRANCISCO, California - Now why doesn't this surprise me coming from San Francisco? City council officials will now have the opportunity to have their sex-change operation covered under their health insurance plan. Mayor Willie Brown and the Board of Supervisors are expected to sign a contract within the next few weeks that will extend a predetermined amount of money in benefits. San Francisco would apparently be the first governmental body in the U.S. to make sex-change benefits available.

Archaeologists Expose 'Drinking Penis' at Museum

LONDON, England - Archaeologists have exposed a "Drinking Penis" at the Museum of London which was found during a dig in the city's outskirts. The phallic-shaped cup is believed to date from the late Stuart period and is being hailed as the only known example of its kind. The cup features life-like testicles and an "anatomically correct" opening at the end. Its original maker also added a small cup above the base and covered it with floral designs in blue and purple. According to Hazel Forsyth, curator of the museum's late collection, the piece reflected the period's "rather bawdy sense of humor" but is also in remarkably good condition.

Disciplinary Action Lands Teacher in Hot Water

NARATHIWAT, Thailand - A teacher in Thailand landed in a "wee" bit of trouble after admitting she ordered five boys to drink their own urine. The group of 10 and 11-year-old boys supposedly admitted to Somporn Khunkliang that they left a urine-filled bottle outside their classroom. The teacher punished the boys by making them drink the urine. Khunkliang is now under investigation by education officials and disciplinary action against her has yet to be announced.

Eenie, Meenie, Miney, Blow

NORTH BERGEN, New Jersey - These kids really know how to work and play well together. A group of 14 and 15-year-old high school students engaged in a game of "Dare" in their classroom during which acts of oral sex and fondling took place. Apparently it was a study period and while their teacher sat at her desk doing paperwork, the group of nine students got into a circle and did their sex education homework. School officials said they are concerned that such activity could take place in school - especially right in a classroom. The teacher has been removed from classroom duty while an investigation ensues. She faces probable disciplinary action.

Dung Shower Makes A Splash On Utah Home

SALT LAKE CITY, Utah - The feces definitely hit the fan and every other part of a home in Utah. A shower of dung from a reportedly unknown source covered two sides of the home, the backyard and a hot tub. When similar blobs hit homes in Salt Lake County in the spring of 1999, homeowners blamed aircraft for dumping septic tanks in flight. But in this last incident, the mess was devoid of tell-tale blue chemicals used in planes' toilets, and officials from the Federal Aviation Administration maintain that aircraft do not have the ability to empty their tanks while flying.

Officials Say It's Ok for Virgins to Go Bananas

RUSSIA - The Russian Banana Party has been going a little fruity for years. They are now backing a policy that makes it Ok to use carrots, bananas and other fruit and vegetables in bed. In Russia, ritualistic intercourse using what they referred to as a "bone knob" had been previously abandoned. However, after being informed that HIV could not be transmitted by infected bananas, the ruling council of the All-

Russian Banana Party decided Russians are now allowed to rightfully use bananas for any purpose. And ironically enough, their mandate went into effect on International Women's Day.

Meeting in the Delivery Room

BOSTON, Massachusetts - "The Most Dedicated Employee" award definitely goes to Massachusetts Republican Governor Jane Swift. The 36-year-old was due to have twins and began having contractions shortly before a scheduled meeting. Though the contractions were coming every six to eight minutes, she wanted to work as long as possible and held the meeting via speaker phone in the hospital. While the pains subsided, Swift signed papers, took other calls, and met with aides, all still under her doctor's supervision. Spokesperson Jason Kauppi said, "She would not describe this as the optimal situation. But if she can continue her job she will. She may be distracted while giving birth." Swift will be the first governor in American history to give birth while in office.

Hell Through Tantalizing Itches

The porn industry is one of the most competitive, especially in Japan where fetish is an art form and thousands of movies are made each year. This competition has forced producers to go to further and further extremes as in the case of one recent hit, "Hell Through Tantalizing Itches." Unlike many other movies of the genre, this film focuses less on sex and more on a guy trying to catch mosquitoes. When he finally has a jar full, it's time for the lady's role. The young woman is bound and blindfolded and the jar of mosquitoes is applied to her breasts. The fun starts when she tries to itch herself. This is just one of the new generation of fetish films. Another entitled "Bicycle Masturbation" follows a woman riding a bicycle with a vibrating seat. As her arousal grows she finds it harder to pedal until she falls over.

No Fuzz For Phony Cop

When is a cop not a cop? When he's a con man trying to blackmail an undercover police officer into having sex. Canadian Trevor Blair Roszell thought he had a pretty good scam. He would pretend to be a plainclothes police officer and demand free sex from prostitutes. There was no way to tell how long he was doing this, but when he propositioned a real undercover cop posing as a prostitute, his free enterprise ended. "During the conversation, he indicated he was a police officer himself and flashed some police paraphernalia to back it up," said prosecutor Joan Blaine. One of two detectives who arrested Roszell said he told the undercover officer he wanted free sex or a reduced rate at the very least.

Pakistani Lifts Heavy Weights in the Blink of an Eye

PUNJAB, Pakistan - Eyelids are said to be heavy at times, but rarely do they become heavy weightlifters. Mahammed Sabir Sipra has trained himself to lift weights using only his eyelids and challenges anyone to lift more. Sipra supposedly came across this talent by accident, while applying 'Surma', a black herbal powder used in Pakistan, to protect his eyes. He accidentally stuck a needle through his eyelid and was surprised at the lid's strength. The idea struck him to lift weights. Sipra warns others "not to try this at home" because he "doesn't want to become responsible for any loss to anybody's eyes."

Miss Israel To Illustrate Bullet Dodging Talent

ISRAEL - Some women get accused of stuffing their bras to win a beauty pageant, but this is a little ridiculous. Miss Israel will wear a bulletproof gown to next month's Miss Universe beauty pageant. In an effort for a more "softer look", the top of the silk dress, embroidered with diamonds and pearls, is covered by an army-issue flak jacket adorned with diamonds. According to designer Galit Levi, the dress sends a message that everyday life should go on despite renewed violence. "I want people in Israel to continue to go out, but to be careful," Levi concluded.

IBM Paying The Price For Advertising Space

CHICAGO, Illinois - IBM may have to pay thousands of dollars in fines and restitution for graffiti spraypainted on Chicago sidewalks in a multimillion-dollar ad campaign. As part of the promotion, softball-sized peace symbols, hearts and penguins appeared on sidewalks in roughly 100 locations, angering local businesses. The advertising company apparently hired 20-year-old Ali Morsy to run around the city at night with a paint can and stencil the images in strategic locations. Debbie DeLopez, who runs the city's graffiti-removal program, said, "It's surprising that a reputable company did something like this." IBM has also run into similar graffiti problems in San Francisco.

God Has Spoken: You Will Be a Vegetable

ROSEDALE, Maryland - One would think God wants us to help the homeless, feed the poor, become doctors, teachers and more. But not Kenny Carter, 40, who is an ex-drug dealer and self-admitted pimp. After spending time in jail and rehabilitation, Carter turned to the church for guidance. During one service Carter described, "I was crying out in the middle of church: 'Oh, God! Oh, God!' And suddenly I heard an audible male voice that said, 'You will be a vegetable.'" That was all Carter needed to hear and asked his friend to make him a pepper costume. He created songs and a vegetable persona called "Peppy the Pepper" and asked his manager at Super Fresh, where he is a community relations manager, if he could try it out on the customers. The company loved the idea, and Peppy the Pepper has been making appearances at different branches ever since.

Warm Mother's Day Wishes Inside and Out

CEDAR CREST, New Mexico - Most mothers may prefer flowers and candy for Mother's Day, but how about a picture of a uterus? The seller, identified only as Voodoogal, claims that an internal photograph of her uterus, complete with Fallopian tubes, would make the perfect Mother's Day present. On the eBay website, she describes the uterus as: "probably the most wonderful organ in the human body, but I am a little biased because I am a woman!"

And Speaking of Practical Jokes...

ARIZONA - Two schoolgirls eagerly volunteered to bake a cake for their Estrella Mountain Elementary School carnival in Arizona. The good deed was to be the prize in one of the carnival competitions. But instead of flour, eggs and sugar the girls used dog excrement, pond water, and laxatives to make the batter. The girls were nice enough, however, to top the cake with whipped cream and Snickers bars. Something (probably the smell) must have alerted officials, and the "treat" was confiscated before anyone could eat any. The girls were questioned and could be charged with conspiracy to commit assault. The offending prize was taken to a laboratory for ingredient analysis.

Stuffing Her Bra Has Whole New Meaning

BEVERLY HILLS, California - You've heard of the Wonderbra, the Miracle Bra, and even the Water Bra, but now comes an undergarment that will stop them cold: the SuperBra. The $30 design is available in black or white, and its unique feature is a holster for a .38 caliber snub-nose revolver. The inventor, Paxton Quigley, said, "Women like the idea of comfort and its ease of access. If a woman is attacked, the purse is the first thing taken from her. A good place to conceal a weapon is in the chest area." Who can argue with that logic?
[I have an idea where she can hide extra bullets.]

Take This Job and Shovel It

NIZHNI NOVGOROD, Russia - And you thought your wages were crappy. Hospital workers in Russia have been offered manure in lieu of their monthly wages. This deal, which is directed at 400 staff members in Nizhni Novgorod, comes out to six tons of manure for the senior doctors. This evidentially is not the first time the staff has partaken in some sort of barter system for their services. They have previously been paid in meat and butter and a group of loggers were reportedly paid in tampons for the whole year of 1994. However, the staff members are terribly offended by this latest offer.

Masturbators Lend a Hand To U.S. Charities

Masturbators are picking up "Good Vibrations" all over the country. The Good Vibration Association has organized a Masturbate-A-Thon as part of National Masturbation Month. Proceeds will go to sexual health charities all across the U.S. Registered participants called their friends and family to sponsor them per minute of masturbation. According The Good Vibration Association's website, "sexual pleasure is a birthright" and their aim is to create a "clearer masturbation conscience." National Masturbation Month ends with a celebration at Oakland's Parkway Theatre in California.

And Stay Out!

The Michigan Senate expelled one of its own Thursday. It was the first time the legislative body has ousted a sitting senator in state history. David Jaye was kicked out of the state Senate following allegations which included drunken driving, putting topless pictures of his fiancee on his Senate computer, beating his fiancee and swearing at his staff. Jaye labeled the inquiry a "railroad job." The rest of the Senate described him as a liar and a bully.

Students See Teacher Masturbate

FLORIDA - Students at Oak Grove Middle School in Florida got more than they bargained for when they borrowed a videotape from their teacher. The instructor, Bernard G. Tschiderer, gave them a tape so they could film scenes for a school project, but apparently "forgot" the tape showed him masturbating. When the students went to view their work, they allegedly saw the teacher in action. According to Michael Bessette, an administrator in the district's office of professional standards, the tape also shows the teacher on his bed wearing only boxers with a cat on his lap. Tschiderer has decided to retire, and police are looking into the situation to determine if a crime was committed.

Two Strikes for Toyota with Black Community

Toyota is taking heat from Jesse Jackson and the Rainbow/PUSH Coalition because of an ad featuring a close-up of an African-American man with a wide smile and a gold image of Toyota's RAV4 SUV on his front tooth. Toyota said the ad was intended to appeal to a "youthful, hip audience through an edgy style statement." But Jackson said the ad was offensive and insensitive and called for a boycott of Toyota dealerships. Last year, the same ad agency angered some African-Americans when it ran an ad in black publications that said, "Unlike your boyfriend, Toyota gets up every morning." Those ads were canceled.

Distributors See Nothing Wrong With Invisible Doll

LONDON, England - Why couldn't this have come out of the ShagMail think tank? A toy firm in England is literally making money out of thin air with its latest doll for children, called "Invisible Jim." The action figure is nothing but an empty packet and is sold around the world by U.S. firm What-If-Atlas-Got-An-Itchy-Bum Company for a few dollars. The packaging reads: "Invisible Jim. As not seen on TV." The blurb goes on: "Batteries not included. A gripping hand would be nice. Camouflage suit sold separately. Includes other great features apparently." Representatives at Trading Standards said this product is perfectly legitimate because as long as people can see that the package is empty and are still willing to pay for it, then no laws are broken.

2000 Pose Nude for "Art" in Montreal

MONTREAL, Canada - When New-York-based Spencer Tunick, 34, asked for volunteers to be photographed nude for Montreal's Museum of Contemporary Arts, he expected about 300 responses. He was ecstatic when over 2,000 undressed for him in 55-degree weather. Tunick's niche is photographs of nude crowds in urban centers, and his works have been displayed all over the world. In Montreal, police set up a barrier to keep out clothed onlookers and supervised the almost hour-long photo shoot. The artist was delighted as he addressed local newspaper reps and said, "This was the easiest performance of this scale that I have done. Here people just listened, they cared about my work and wanted to be part of something original."

Penis Show Has Some Swansea People Scared Stiff

SWANSEA, Wales - The residents of Swansea are conflicted over the upcoming sold-out presentation "Puppetry of the Penis" to be held at the Grand Theatre. In the show, two Australians "shape" their genitals to look like various landmarks and objects. While the show is sold out, over 400 people have petitioned for the show to be stopped, claiming it is immoral. Swansea Council's culture secretary Robert Francis-Davies said, "I know that some people say the show next month is pornographic, but it has been featured at the Edinburgh Festival and London's West End. People have the right to go or not go, and if they feel offended they should stay away."

Teaspoon of Ketchup Makes Heinz's Profits go Down

SHASTA COUNTY, California - An ounce and a half of missing ketchup was hard for the Heinz Corporation to swallow. Bill and Marcia Baker discovered their 20 oz. bottle was underfilled by the aforementioned proportion while baking five years ago. They called the local council which spurred a five-year investigation by weights and measures. Officials found millions of bottles under-filled. The company has agreed to pay Shasta County, where the complaint originated, $180,000. They also agreed to overfill the bottles for a year which will cost the company an additional $650,000.

Killer's Body Used in Art Exhibit

LONDON, England - London art student Marilene Oliver was intrigued by the idea of downloading images of a deceased man from the Internet. The fact that the man was put to death in 1993 for killing a pensioner is irrelevant she says. Joseph Jernigan was executed by lethal injection and donated his body to science. His corpse was cut into a thousand slices and photographed for the Internet. In her art exhibit "I Know You Inside Out," Oliver used the printed images and placed them on stacked sheets of plastic to create a life-sized figure of the murderer. Her other piece, "I Know Every Inch of Your Body," will be displayed right by it. The latter will be a touch screen digital image of the artist's flayed skin. According to Oliver, the two pieces are just like Adam and Eve.

Transsexual has Plan to Fund Sex Change Operation

PORTLAND, Oregon - A transsexual in Portland, Oregon, tells researchers they can test her testes all they want as long as they help her pay to become a woman. Sherri LeAnn De Rossett, 56, says she has spent all of her life as a woman trapped in a man's body and has been unable to live the life she considers normal. Rossett went on to say that while her testes are no longer of any use to her, they could be used to help others through the use of medical research instead of being thrown away when removed. Rossett's loyal wife Grecia, to whom she has been married for 30 years, and their three children, have been very supportive of her plight. She has now started her hormone therapy and the next step is the surgery, which she expects to have in 2002 and should cost around $20,000.

Is Your Life Worth a Doughnut?

HOUSTON, Texas - An ambulance driver caused alarm when he stopped for doughnuts en route to the hospital with a patient in his vehicle. This event, coupled with several other similar incidences, prompted the Texas Health Department to begin an official investigation last February into the Houston Fire Department. The Department was put on a one-year probation and told they had to hire someone to oversee certification or pay a $33,000 fine. This penalty did not serve the intended purpose, however, because the Fire Department was in trouble again the following month when an ambulance driver transported former Mayor Bob Lanier to the hospital in an unlicensed vehicle.

100-year-Old Earns College Degree

MISSOURI VALLEY, Iowa - An Iowa woman received a very special present on her 100th birthday - her college diploma. Myrtle Thomas taught for 20 years at a time when a high school diploma was all that was needed. She took college courses for her bachelor's degree in education at the University of Nebraska at Omaha. But to get her diploma she would have been required to quit teaching to do 16 weeks of student teaching. Dean of Education, John Christensen, recently met with others at the college, and they decided to waive the student-teaching requirement in this case.

Art 101: Masturbation Lessons?

WINNIPEG, Canada - Teenage girls in Canada who attended a Women in Art course at the University of Winnipeg were treated with lessons on how to masturbate with vegetables instead. John Carlyle, who runs the River East division where the girls studied, stressed that the videos shown to the girls contained no nudity, but the "actresses" demonstrated how bananas, cucumbers, carrots, and more could sexually pleasure them. Parents revolted after hearing about the content, and according to Carlyle, "By the end of the first day, the phone calls from parents were just deafening." The University's president, Constance Rooke, agreed the material was inappropriate for the 15-year-old students and said it would not happen again.

Brazilian Sperm Bank Needs a Hand

SAO PAULO, Brazil - Reserves are dangerously low in Sao Paulo, Brazil. Sperm reserves, that is. To help boost "donations," the Department of Human Reproduction at the Albert Einstein Hospital has launched an aggressive campaign. In one advertisement, a baby boy holds a *Playboy* magazine with the following tagline under it: "Give it a hand so that he can be born." Worried about the depleting sources, coordinators are hoping the *Playboy* ads will draw more attention. Fertility specialist Dr. Jorge Hallack explained the urgency: "Nine in ten potential donors are rejected, so in order to have a reasonable stock of good semen, we need to research the semen of at least 1,500 men."

Brawl Breaks Out on the Golf Course

SPARTANBURG, South Carolina - A group of four men went to the Village Greens golf course for a friendly round of golf one afternoon. The game turned vicious, however, when three of them asked the fourth player, Victor Earley, 39, to leave because of his annoying behavior. Early left, but quickly returned in a golf cart to play behind the group and harass them. A fist fight ensued, during which Early swung a golf club at one of the men, Paul Hughes. In retaliation, Hughes pulled out a hunting knife and cut Earley across the chest. Hughes has been charged with serious assault and battery for the offense, and Lt. Ron Gahagan said, "The impression the officers had is that they really didn't like this guy, but they decided to let him play because he is related to one of them in some capacity."

Irishmen Take Their Guinness Seriously

DUBLIN, Ireland - Workers laid off when a Guinness packaging plant closes will be able to drown their sorrows in beer, thanks to a severance package that includes up to 10 years' free supply of the famous stout. "It is a tradition within the [brewing] industry that employees get a beer allowance, amounting to about two bottles a day," said Pat Barry, director of corporate affairs for Guinness Ireland. The number of years workers receive the beer allowance will depend on years of service, he said, adding that the size of the payment also will depend on length of employment, with workers receiving an average payout of about $70,000.

German Madonna Fans Get More Buck for the Bang

BERLIN - A German website has offered Madonna fans a ticket for a sold-out concert in Berlin in exchange for having sex with one of its reporters. The web publisher Bernd Heusinger said 22 readers have applied for a chance to win the ticket including 12 males, six females and four homosexual readers. "There's nothing illegal about it," Heusinger said. "No one is being forced to take part." The Madonna concerts in Berlin were sold out within minutes of going on sale and went for record prices, by German standards, of up to $110 each.

Oops, They Did It Again...and Got Fired

DALLAS, Texas - Two Dallas disc jockeys, Keith Kramer and Tony Longo (aka Kramer & Twitch from the "Extreme Night Time Radio" show), fabricated a story about pop princess Britney Spears and her NSync boyfriend Justin Timberlake being in an accident. They reported Spears died, while Timberlake remained in a coma. Shortly after, the Los Angeles police and fire department were swamped with calls from fans and news reporters trying to confirm the story. The disc jockeys were later fired for the hoax even though they claim to have had clearance to run the story from the program director. Meanwhile, a spokesman for Jive Records have said representatives of Spears and Timberlake are considering legal action against the DJs.

Man Throws Loveable Puppet A Smack Down

LANGHORNE, Pennsylvania - Lee McPhatter's three-year-old daughter Mina was going to take a picture with the Cookie Monster at the Sesame Place theme park, whether the Cookie Monster wanted to or not. When the woman inside the fuzzy blue suit tried to push the little girl aside, McPhatter supposedly pushed her to the ground and kicked her in the head and back. People started yelling at him for brutalizing the lovable children's entertainer, but McPhatter says he did not kick or punch the Cookie Monster. That is not the story of actress Jennie McNelis who police say suffered bruised ribs and a cervical sprain.

62-year-old Has Brother's Baby

FRANCE - A 62-year-old woman caused a commotion in France last month when she became the oldest known woman to give birth. Back in the news again, the woman claims the father of her baby girl is her brother. The woman, Jeanine, underwent invitro fertilization in the United States, using the egg of an American woman and, reportedly, sperm donated by her 52-year-old brother, Robert. "I could no longer transmit my genetic inheritance because of my age," Jeanine told Le Parisien newspaper. "So I wanted to transmit his, and give birth so our (genetic) line would continue." She told the newspaper she had no regrets about her decision to have a test-tube baby with her brother. "I have not committed any moral error in my pursuit, and I have no problem with my conscience," she told the paper. No news yet if she will appear on Jerry Springer.

Canadian Phone Company Tells Woman Touch This

TORONTO, Canada - Representatives at Bell Canada reached out to a woman - to give her a $5,000 phone bill. Dianna Freiesleben from Oshawa, near Toronto, was slapped with the hefty fee after she let her home computer dial up a work number for more than a week. Freiesleben, who works at home transcribing medical records for a Toronto hospital, says she was completely flabbergasted when she got a call from an "unfriendly" customer service representative at Bell Canada. She reluctantly worked out a monthly payment plan with the telephone company, but says she has "learned a costly lesson."

No Mustard or Relish, Please

NEW YORK, New York - For a long time the record in Nathan's annual frankfurter-eating contest stood at 25 weenies in just six minutes, 13 seconds. But this year the old record was broken, no, shattered by Takeru Kobayashi of Japan who, in his first-ever attempt at the contest, swallowed an incredible 50 hot dogs in just 12 minutes. That's complete with buns, folks. Eyewitnesses said it was by far the most amazing performance since the annual Fourth of July contest began way back in 1916. By the end of the 12-minute event, the rest of the 19-member field had stopped eating to watch. Kobayashi measures a modest 5-foot-7, 131-pounds.

Students Can't Cheat and Attack Professor

PATNA, India - Trouble began on a college campus near Patna, the capital of the eastern Indian state. School officials seized books and notes from 18 students about to take an exam, and the students boycotted the test in retaliation. Angry at not being able to cheat, a group of students later attacked veterinary college principal Mani Mohan Prasad. They threw gasoline bombs at his car, and the professor suffered burns to 30% of his body. According to police, the students on motorcycles were armed with everything from hockey sticks and knives to revolvers and petrol bombs. Prasad said, "The students rained hockey sticks on me. I then managed to extricate myself and got in the car, but the car was also attacked by the marauders with petrol bombs." Two students were arrested, and the school was closed indefinitely.

Sex Shop: A Threat to Society

PHNOM PENH, Cambodia - The only Cambodian sex shop was closed the day after it opened when police confiscated boxes of rubber penises and vaginas, condoms, batteries, and assorted Chinese aphrodisiacs. All were said to be a danger to women and threat to the Cambodian society at large. Yuan Genxing, the 38-year-old shop owner, was arrested and charged with debauchery under laws on sex trafficking. If convicted, he faces up to 15 years in jail. According to police Chief Yim Symany, the items "are dangerous to Cambodian womens' health and Cambodian culture. This is very dangerous. Look how large those rubber penises are. There is also medicine to keep sex going longer. If people use this medicine, it could be dangerous for them."

Men and Women Flogged for Dancing

TEHRAN, Iran - You thought *your* parents were strict. Fifty Iranian men and women between the ages of 18 and 25 were rounded up by police for dancing at a party together and were later flogged after a court found them guilty of depravity. The government-run daily newspaper in Iran reports that the partygoers received 30 to 99 lashes after they were arrested last weekend in an apartment in an upper-class district in northern Tehran. The paper quoted the judge as saying that the group was celebrating the birthday of the daughter of the landlord when they were caught dancing together. Mixed parties are banned in Iran on religious grounds and penalties include fines, whipping and prison terms.

Bizarre Practical Joker Fools Doctors And Police

MADRID, Spain - A passerby in the south Spanish town of Armilla found what he thought was a three-month-old fetus on the sidewalk. Emergency services took it to a hospital where two doctors, who gave it a preliminary examination, immediately suspected an illegal abortion. They alerted the police who began a search for the mother. It wasn't until the doctors started an autopsy two days later that they discovered the fetus was a doll. "It was a very real looking doll, covered in liquid," a police spokesman said. "It looks like a joke in very bad taste."

Congratulations: You Have a Bouncing Baby Honda

NEW YORK - Remember back in the day when new parents named their children after relatives or respected individuals in their lives? Evidently these days are long gone. Jason Black and Frances Schroeder are in the process of looking for a corporate sponsor to name the baby boy that they are expecting. "The exposure that it could bring to a business is potentially huge, and we think it would be well worth the investment on their part," Black explained. The expectant couple has put the naming rights up for auction on both eBay and Yahoo!, at a minimum bid of $500,000. The ads ran from July 18 through July 28. There have been no bidders thus far, but they plan to extend their offer.

Skydiver Provided Stiff Competition in Contest

SOUTH AFRICA - Kids, don't try this at home! James Reilly, 36, has won a new car after skydiving naked with a stick of deodorant bound by tape to his genitals. Reilly won first prize in a radio competition for the wackiest act and will receive a Peugeot 206 for his efforts. According to Reilly, "For three minutes of coldness, it was worth it." [Where would this guy stick the deodorant for a million bucks?]

Homeless Could Have Their Own Voicemail Boxes

"I am sorry, I am away from my cardboard box right now, but if you'd leave your name and number I will get back to you as soon as I can..." This may sound like a crazy message for an answering machine, but it could become a reality for homeless individuals in Wisconsin. The 2001-'03 budget now awaiting Gov. Scott McCallum's signature calls for spending $40,000 over the next two years to help set up voice mailboxes for the homeless. Some homeless advocates say voice mail can be a way to bridge the disconnect, a key step toward breaking the cycle of homelessness. Others are opposed to the new budget plan and say that the proposed funds could be used for job skill training or even new bedding for these individuals. Director of Services, Karla Jameson, concluded by saying "Of the 150 Madison people who have used them over the years, there have been plenty of success stories."

Lost and Found: Severed Male Genitals

BANGKOK - This couldn't have happened in a more appropriately-named city. A set of severed male genitals has been found in a rubbish bin in Bangkok. A custodian found the organs in a garbage bin at Siam Square railway station after they were neatly wrapped in a paper napkin, inside a clear plastic wrapper, and placed in a plastic bag.

Police are asking hospitals and police stations if anyone has shown up missing their genitals. The severed organs have since been sent to the Institute of Forensic Medicine for examination.

Couple Forcibly Impregnate Teenage Daughter

AKRON, Ohio - In a bizarre bid for another child, an infertile Ohio woman and her husband forcibly impregnated the woman's daughter with her stepfather's semen. The girl, who was not identified, said when she was 16 her mother, Narda Goff, asked her to bear her husband's child because she has multiple sclerosis and could no longer give birth. The girl claims her parents monitored her menstrual cycle and then used syringes to impregnate her against her will. The Goffs have been charged with rape and sexual battery. Both have pleaded innocent despite paternity tests confirming John Goff is the father of the girl's now 22-month-old son, prosecutors say. The daughter has moved in with her fiance's family. She has given her son to county authorities and hopes an aunt will adopt him. She said she would consider the boy her cousin.

Finding A Good Apartment Is Murder

NEW YORK - Has it ever seemed like every good apartment in the city is taken? It certainly did to 20-year-old Bernard Perez. He apparently cut off one man's head so he and his roommate, Rahman Williams, 21, could move into his Manhattan apartment. Police began to find bits and pieces of the victim all over the neighborhood. The man's hands were found in a plastic bag in a dumpster near the building, and his legs and torso were found about two blocks away. The head was conveniently concealed under the kitchen sink. Perez was also charged with murdering Doris Drakeford, 44, who lived in the same building as the dismembered man in a different apartment. Her body was found in the Harlem River and police said she had been strangled.

Woman In Coma Delivers Baby

CINCINNATI, Ohio - A woman who has been in a coma for eight months gave birth to a healthy, full-term girl. It is one of few known cases in the United States in which a woman was in a coma virtually throughout the gestation period and still carried the pregnancy to term, Dr. Michael Hnat, a neonatologist at University Hospital, said. Chastity Cooper, 24, was about two weeks pregnant when she suffered severe head injuries in a car crash and went into a coma. The birth was aided by labor-inducing medications but no strong pain relievers. The baby girl was named Alexis Michelle.

Tourists Line Up To Be Hot Lunch

ADELAIDE, Australia - It is unusual to see a school of great white sharks feeding in the wild. It is even more unusual to see people clambering on top of a dead whale to actually put their hands on the ravenous flesh-eaters while feeding. But that is exactly what happened near Cape Jervis in Australia. A southern right whale died 60 miles south of Adelaide and about a dozen sharks were soon devouring the carcass. Sightseers were caught on film walking over the dead animal to pet the feeding sharks. "These creatures are not toys," said Environment Minister Iain Evans. "In the case of the great white, they can be extremely dangerous and it is clear the state government will need to look at changing the law in order to protect people too stupid to protect themselves." Miraculously, no one was reported injured.

Man Hires Sex Slave Over the Internet

CANTON, Ohio - You can buy just about anything over the Internet these days, including a sex slave. Kevin Erwin hired a female "sex slave" online, but the state of Ohio has charged him with rape, kidnapping, and assault for his treatment of the woman. In his defense, Erwin provided the police with a signed contact from the woman giving him full authority to use her at his every whim. The woman agreed "to freely give myself to Kevin L. Erwin as a personal slave and life mate" and "to make myself sexually available to Kevin at all times." In addition, she agreed to divorce her husband and marry Erwin. If she ever broke the said contract, she agreed to pay her "master" $100,000. The contract is being contested as the prosecutor insists the woman was coerced.

Student's Sweet Surprise Ends on Sour Note

CHIPPEWA FALLS, Wisconsin - Remember when students used to bring an apple for the teacher? John Smith from Chippewa Falls, Wisconsin took this idea to the extreme when he shaved his body hair and included it in a cake for faculty members. The 18-year-old pleaded guilty to disorderly conduct. He was sentenced to 12 months probation and 120 hours community service. It was not mentioned whether that service would be carried out in the school cafeteria.

Republicans Have More Nightmares

CALIFORNIA - A prominent dream researcher displayed her findings of a recent study this week at the 18th Annual International Conference of the Association for the Study of Dreams in Santa Cruz. Kelly Bulkeley of the Graduate Theological Union in Berkeley, California, concludes that Republicans have scarier and more frequent nightmares than Democrats. In fact, "Half of the dreams of Republicans in my study were classified as nightmares, compared to only about 18 percent of the dreams of Democrats," Bulkeley reports. Both parties are blaming the head honcho. "What do you expect after eight years of William Jefferson Clinton?" Kevin Sheridan, Republican National Committee deputy press secretary, told UPI. "If George W. Bush were the leader of my party, I'd have trouble sleeping at night, too," quipped Democratic National Committee chairman Terry McAuliffe.

Monica Lewinsky Panty Sales "Go Down" in History

CHILE - Crotchless Panty Sales named after the queen of scandalous interns, Monica Lewinsky, are booming in Chile. Entrepreneur Abraham Kuncar Rabah admitted to reporters that the name was intended to be a talking point and to draw attention to his product. A sign tells customers the Lewinsky panties are "always ready". The shopkeeper hopes the reference to the U.S. presidential scandal would cheer people up during the country's recession. "Tourists who pass my shop go crazy. They stop, point at the name, take photos and sometimes film our mannequins. I think I should be exporting internationally," Kuncar concluded.

Romanian Caught with Pants Down in Sex Shop

CLUJ, Romania - A drunken Romanian man took out his sexual frustrastion on a rubber doll after breaking into a sex shop. The 43-year-old unemployed miner had reportedly travelled to Cluj to look for work, but went drinking after failing to find a job. He allegedly smashed the window of a neighborhood sex shop where the doll was on display and started using it on the shop counter. Police claim he was still mumbling into the ear of the doll when they told him to pull up his trousers.

The Secret of Japanese Ass Clenching

TOKYO, Japan - A Japanese author has butted his way into the publishing industry with his new book, *How to Goodbye Depression*. In his book, Hiroyuki Nishigaki claims clenching your anus 100 times a day and pulling in the tummy button 100 times will help combat depression. According to Nishigaki, constricting the anus 100 times and denting the navel 100 times in succession every day is effective and can be done anywhere from a boring meeting to a crowded subway. "I have known a 70-year-old man who has practiced this for 20 years. As a result, he has a good complexion and has grown 20 years younger," he concluded.

No-Fault Litigation Just Getting Silly

TACOMA, Washington - According to a report in the *Tacoma Tribune*, Joshua Harris is suing hypnotist Travis Fox who, he said, caused him to break his hand while under hypnosis. Fox was entertaining audiences at the Puyallup Fair and asked Harris if he wanted to volunteer. Fox then hypnotized him, and by allegedly manipulating his subconscious, caused Harris to believe he was being attacked by aliens. While flailing his arms about, Harris managed to break his hand. He has now filed a personal injury lawsuit alleging negligence by Fox, Fox's manager, the Western Washington Fair Association and the company that booked Fox's act. Harris is seeking unspecified damages for pain and suffering.

[And people are surprised that America has a world-record one lawyer per 295 people.]

Residents Go Bananas Over Monkey Man Sightings

GHAZIBAD, India - "Beware of the Monkey Man" sounds like a title of a new horror movie, but it is an actual cry heard in the streets of Ghazibad, India. Since April, more than a dozen people have reportedly been treated in hospitals for fractures or deep scratches caused by this so called Monkey Man. Police are being bombarded with phone calls about sightings and attacks by this Monkey Man, who some claim is a beast and others a man wearing a rhesus monkey mask. Last week, police arrested a man for wearing a rhesus monkey mask to scare people. However, the attacks and sightings have continued since the suspect's arrest. The latest victim was housewife Shamir Begum, 30, who fainted after she came across the Monkey Man prowling on her terrace. When she came to he had gone.

The British Flying Saucer Bureau Says UF-uh-oh

LONDON, England - Queetzal must be keeping to himself these days. The British Flying Saucer Bureau is closing after chronicling UFO activities for nearly 50 years - because of a sharp decline in the number of reported sightings. The group used to receive at least 30 reports a week of sightings of unidentified flying objects and had approximately 1,500 members worldwide. Now, the sightings have virtually dried up. According to Denis Plunkett, who founded the bureau in 1953 with his late father Edgar, there may be a rational explanation for the decline in sightings. Perhaps alien visitors had completed a survey of the earth.

Woman's Son Reincarnated as a Lizard

NONTHABURI, Thailand - When Chamlong Taengniem's 13-year-old son died in a motorcycle accident, she had no idea he would revisit her. As a lizard. The mother claims a lizard followed her home after her son's cremation and sleeps in his mattress and drinks his favorite drinks. Flocks of people have journeyed to the woman's home to catch a glimpse of the lizard, even stroking its stomach in the hopes of finding clues to future lottery numbers. Out of respect, people left gifts for the lizard as well. People in Buddhist nations generally believe in reincarnation and a spirit's life after death.

Kinky Ghost Has People Under His Spell

ZANZIBAR ISLAND, Africa - The people of Africa have a reason to fear the things that go bump (and grind) in the middle of the night. Rumor has it there is a sexually-aggressive ghost that attacks people while they are asleep. The ghost goes by the name of Popo Bawa and people say he prefers to visit sleepers while they are in their own beds at home. Popo's presence is said to be revealed by an acrid smell and a puff of smoke. Women, however, are less concerned about this supernatural threat than the local men because this particular spirit has a preference for men, many of whom have reported being sodomized while they were asleep.

Artist Beams With A Heap of Pride

LONDON - This will be one prize artist David Shepherd will surely never forget. Shepherd, who is famed for his paintings of elephants, is to be given a trophy made from elephant dung for his 70th birthday. The award will be presented to Shepherd with the glazed and engraved droppings at London's Natural History Museum. A spokesman for Shepherd's conservation trust told reporters, "It is a humorous offering for a man who likes to see the funny side of everything."

Drunken Partygoer Causes Hairy Situation for Police

AMSTERDAM, Netherlands - Dutch police approached with caution what appeared to be a brown bear slumbering on the side of the road. Disturbing a sleeping bear can be dangerous business. But this particular carnivore turned out to be a drunken human in a bear suit. The man had overindulged at what we can only assume was a costume party and decided to walk home in his bear outfit. He had barely made it onto the road before collapsing in an alcoholic stupor, giving the local police a story to tell in the squad room for years to come.

One From the Truth in Advertising Archives

In 1995, Pizza Hut scheduled a commercial featuring Pete Rose. According to news reports, "a young boy is supposed to ask Pete about his accomplishments in baseball. At the end, Rose asks if the boy likes Pizza Hut pizza, and the boy replies, 'You bet!'" After reviewing the script, the company canceled the script. "That's not the best choice of words," explained Rose.

Testicle Theft Is No Bull in Canada

EDMONTON - I have heard of taking the bull by the horns, but this is ridiculous. Edmonton police are searching for vandals who sliced the testicles off 20 fiberglass bison. The life-sized models were placed around the streets of Edmonton as decoration for the World Athletics Championships. Police reportedly have no suspects for the theft at this time and are baffled towards the motive. "It's certainly not for money. I mean, what can someone get for testicles? I don't think there's a market for that," concluded police spokesman Dean Parthenis.

Stone Cold Claims Abduction

WWF Champion "Stone Cold" Steve Austin is the latest celebrity to claim he was abducted by space aliens. After missing for six days, Austin told police, "They said they came to Earth in peace, they love wrestling and they just wanted to meet me." Austin further stated that he did not remember much of the six-day ordeal.
[Queetzal, if you are reading, can you shed any light on this highly credible report?]

"Gesundheit!"

ENGLAND - The Australian Broadcasting Corporation Newsdesk reports the incredible case of a blind woman who regained her sight after suffering a prolonged sneezing fit. 97-year-old Gladys Adamson, who lives near Cambridge, England, had been almost blind for about five years. For some unknown reason she was seized by a bizarre sneezing fit. One morning, the next week, she stood in front of her bathroom mirror and saw her reflection. A health care charity, which had been working with Mrs. Adamson for several years, says it had never known a case like it. Adamson described her sudden recovery as a miracle.

Freaky Circus Sex Just Isn't Funny

RIVERHEAD, New York - A professional circus clown has been convicted of sodomizing his teenage assistant. Christopher Bayer, 29, known as "Smiley the Clown," was found guilty on nine counts including sodomy, sexual abuse and endangering the welfare of a child. He was acquitted on four other charges. Bayer said he would appeal.

Amorous Couple Gets Caught In Sticky Situation

IPOH, Malaysia - Sexual activity can often form a certain bond between a couple, but it usually doesn't take a medical team to break that bond. This was not the case for two lovers who got stuck together during sex and had to be rushed naked to hospital by ambulance. The couple could not pull apart when the 50-year-old woman became "abnormally excited" after taking a sexual stimulant similar to Viagra. The amorous couple reportedly panicked when they could not disengage themselves and called upon neighbors for help. The couple then had to be carried to the ambulance like a pair of "Siamese Twins" joined together at their private parts.

2

Weird Science

If we look down the well of history we will see, at every water-mark, the indelible mark of technology. The first farmer to break the ground with a plow, the first metallurgist to mix copper and tin, the first engineer to harness the power of steam. Each innovation marks a evolution in mankind's development. It is the single most influential element in human history, so it is no wonder that this book should devote a chapter to the bizarre side of technology? Why shouldn't the self-heating underpants stand next to the internal combustion engine? Why should the telegraph get more fame than the prosthetic chin? This chapter will give you the opportunity to decide for yourself.

New Garment Aimed to Give Women Extra Boost

JAPAN - For those looking for an extra vitamin C boost throughout the day, this could be the product for you. The Fuji Spinning Company in Japan has reportedly developed a T-shirt containing a chemical which turns into vitamin C when it touches human skin. The T-shirt is said to be made out of fiber called V-up, and has the equivalent vitamin content of two lemons. It would also remain effective after 30 washes. According to representatives from the company, the product should be available as early as next year and there are also plans for vitamin-enhanced lace underwear. The company also produces fibers with anti-odor and anti-bacterial properties derived from catechin, a substance extracted from the shells of crabs and shrimp.

Next Jerry Springer: You Thought You Were a Boy

NAIROBI, Kenya - A teenage boy complaining of stomach pains was taken to a hospital only to find out that he was actually a girl. The pains he felt were menstrual cramps. A district medical officer at Meru General Hospital explained that the 18 year old had a vagina, but did not realize it because of a membrane covering it. It is unclear if he thought this membrane was a penis. The boy inherently felt more feminine and subsequently underwent a sex change operation. Dr. Ogange, the patient's physician, said he and the family would go through extensive therapy. The boy would only be released from the hospital after such counseling. This was only the second sex change operation ever conducted in Kenya.

British Army Boasts Best-Stacked Soldiers

LONDON - In an effort to make a happier, bustier soldier, the British army has paid for a number of its female personnel to have breast enlargements, the Ministry of Defense said. And it's not even just officers. In one case, a 27-year-old corporal underwent cosmetic surgery worth $3,600, courtesy of the armed forces. A ministry spokesman defended the policy, saying that surgery would only be paid for if there was an overriding physical or psychological reason to do so. [Like having small breasts.]

The Cutting Edge of Medical Science

HOUSTON, Texas - A new, non-surgical breast enlargement gadget will be available in the United States this month. The Brava system focuses mainly on a computerized bra that the woman must wear ten hours a day for ten weeks. The two plastic cups, which reportedly induce cell growth, are linked to a computer. The cups pull the breast tissue like the suction of a vacuum. The system will cost from $2,000 to $2,500, and according to a doctor overseeing the testing, each participant experienced an increase in cup size. Cathy Martin, who has been testing the device, told the WFAA website in Texas: "There was a difference after having three kids and so, after wearing the bra, it was like before kids."
[Combined with a vibrating massager, a woman would never have to leave the house.]

"Can I Buy You a Wunder Titte?"

SWEDEN - A new Swedish soft drink that claims it can increase the size of a woman's breasts will soon hit American stores. The gold-colored drink is called "Wunder Titte" - German for "Wonderful Breasts." A spokesman for importer Nordic Drinks says women who drink the tonic for at least four months can expect to increase their busts by up to one full cup size. The drink contains special herbs that supposedly stimulate female hormones. It will sell for about $3 per 8-ounce can - mostly in health food stores, bars, and night clubs.
[I'm sure it will be a hit in nightclubs... "Hi there. I'd offer to buy you a Wunder Titte, but I see you already drink it."]

Up the Creek With A Paddle and Two Buoys

PHILADELPHIA - Should they call her "Bubba" or "Bubbette?" A judge has ruled that Patricia Colleen McGrath, formerly Richard Patrick McGrath, who has a penis and D-cup breasts, may be jailed in a women's prison. McGrath was convicted in February 2000 for twice robbing a bank in Bucks County at gunpoint. U.S. District Judge Jan DuBois agreed the 66 year old should go to a prison medical facility but should be jailed with other women if ever released from the institution. Defense lawyer Maranna Meehan argued the intersexual bank robber would be at risk in a male prison, while prosecutors claim she could be a threat to women because of her male genitalia.

Condoms Have Indian Weavers In Stitches

VARANSI, India - Condoms aren't just for safe sex anymore. At least not in India. Sari-makers in Veransi are using lubricated condoms to speed up their weaving and to stop the yarn from snapping. Workers rub the condoms on bobbins while they make their brocade saris. This lubricant is said to smooth the bobbin and makes it move faster between threads. Estimates show that each of the 125,000 looms in the the city uses an average four condoms per day. It takes nearly 15 condoms to produce one Benarasi sari.

[But no condoms at all to produce a new Benarasi sari wearer.]

Inventor Puts Menstruating Women in the Hot Seat

STOCKHOLM, Sweden - How do you spell relief? Swedish inventor Per Wallin hopes menstruating women all over the world will use heated underpants to spell relief. According to Wallin, these garments use chemical pads which generate their own heat and stay warm for up to an hour before they need to be replaced. This warmth provides pain relief as an alternative to painkillers. The hot pants recently won a local innovation prize in southern Sweden, making the invention a candidate for a $37,000 Swedish crown national scholarship. Wallin says he is now looking for an investor to manufacture these underpants on a large scale.

New Back Procedure a Source for Orgasms

WASHINGTON - Who would have ever thought that undergoing treatment for chronic back pain could be such an orgasmic experience? A female patient of North Carolina surgeon Stuart Meloy certainly changed her tune as she received an orgasm while the doctor placed pain-relieving electrodes in her spine. The patient was reportedly conscious throughout the operation so she could help him find the right spot, but when she started shouting it was for all the wrong reasons. She then told Meloy, "You'll have to teach my husband to do that." The good doctor is going above and beyond that step by working on a hand-held remote-control device that will be able to trigger an orgasm at the push of a button. The only drawback, according to Meloy, is that the device is as invasive as a pacemaker and should only be used for extreme cases."

Germ Could Give Men A G'Day With Their Mate

AUSTRALIA - Fertility experts have discovered something new on the "Down Under" regions of critters from Australia. Scientists are trying to find out whether a germ found in the penis of a koala bear may be used to help couples who are having difficulty having children. These germs reportedly live in a sac where the marsupial stores its penis and may cause problems that are only treatable by antibiotic treatment. If a similar germ is found in men, scientists will know more about what causes some types of infertility in humans and could be one step closer to finding a cure.

Phone Company Tries to Stimulate New Customers

NETHERLANDS - Instead of reaching out to "touch someone," a Dutch telephone dealership is encouraging customers to touch themselves. When a person orders a subscription to telephone company KPN with Tring, they are reportedly given a free Nokia phone and a sex toy. Both Nokia and KPN are said to be disgusted with the promotion and are encouraging Tring to drop the deal.

Potential Customer for that Urine Salesman?

INDONESIA - An apple a day apparently isn't the only thing that will keep the doctor away. According to Iwan Budiarso, 68, drinking and bathing in your own urine can fight the aging process. This urine therapy supposedly can cure a variety of illnesses, including cancer, as well as restore hair and reduce wrinkles. The pensioner claims to have used the therapy to help three previously infertile couples to conceive and says novices should mix their first few drinks with equal amounts of water. He concluded by stating that his own personal catchphrase is, "One cup a day keeps you healthy and gay, three cups a day keep diseases away, five cups a day keep your cancer away."

Turning Shit into Gold

WASHINGTON - The Department of Energy has authorized an $800,000 grant for scientists to extract productive chemicals from animal feces. The latter generally contains carbohydrates, proteins, fiber, mineral matter, rocks, and more, and researchers hope to use the carbs and protein to make such chemicals as diols and glycols. These chemicals can be used in antifreeze and various types of plastic. In effect, the positive aspects could counterbalance the need for some harmful products like petroleum-based chemicals. The whole process could make money in the long run: feces cost one to two cents per pound, but extracted chemicals would be worth 20-30 cents per pound.

Doctor Has 'Scoop' on Medicinal Cockroach Dung

THAILAND - A doctor claims that babies' mouth ulcers may be cured using cockroach feces. Dr. Kanvee Viwatpanich of the National Institute of Thai Traditional Medicine, has found references to insect-based remedies in ancient texts and has been advised by different healers on the topic. They instructed him to heat the dung and rub it into the sores of newborn babies. Dr. Viwatpanich truly believes cockroaches have the most medicinal potential. He told reporters, "It was very distinctly used in the past, has survived for thousands of years and has some very good properties."

Designer Has Brief Solution For Chronic Flatulence

DENVER, Colorado - Whoever said charcoal was just for grilling out evidently never heard of fart-proof underwear. 62-year-old inventor Buck Weimer from Colorado has reportedly designed a pair of air-tight undies with a replaceable charcoal filter to remove bad gas before it escapes. Weimer apparently thought up the flatulent-fighting invention, which he named Under-Ease, after his wife "let go a bomb" in bed one night. Buck explained the removable filter - which looks similar to the shoulder pads placed in women's clothing - is made of charcoal sandwiched between two layers of Australian sheep's wool. They sell for $24.95 over the Internet.

Scientists Breathe New Life into Smelly Subject

AUSTRALIA - Scientists are hard at work proving once and for all farting's harmful effects on the environment. Bacteria were said to have been found growing all over a laboratory dish after the research team had a boy break wind on it. The team is now looking for sponsorship from a baked bean manufacturer or curry maker to help fund their research. The journal *New Scientist* welcomed the research, said to help shed light on this little-known threat to public health.

Don't Forget To Feed The Laundry

MASSACHUSETTS - In probably the grossest scientific development since the fecal enema, biotechnologists at the University of Massachusetts are experimenting with fibers implanted with a strain of Escherichia coli that will consume dirt and human sweat. That's right- living clothes that clean themselves. When the food runs out, the bacteria can be reactivated with nutrients, they hope. For the self-cleaning shirt, it means you would only have to wear the garment and sweat it up a little in order bring the bacteria back to life. "You could end up having to feed your shirt instead of wash it," one researcher said.

Ground-Up Fish to Help With Environment

MADISON, Wisconsin - A scientist at the University of Wisconsin is finding a way to "beat the carp" out of the disposable diaper industry. Srinivasan Damodaran has patented a process that turns ground-up fish into an absorbent, biodegradable gel that can be used in diapers. A regular disposable diaper reportedly containing a crystal or powder absorbs 100 times its own weight in water, whereas Damodaran claims his product absorbs 400 times its weight. In addition, the fish- based gel deteriorates in landfills within 28 days, while most diaper gels made from petroleum usually break down much more slowly. Wisconsin officials say they are hoping the product is successful because their waterways are overpopulated with carp.

Scientists Create Robo-Fish

CHICAGO, Illinois - Actual Cyborgs are one step closer with the cre- ation of a robot that is controlled by a fish brain. According to this week's *New Scientist*, scientists at Northwestern University in Chicago, along with colleagues at the University of Genoa in Italy, built the creature while exploring how brain cells adapt to changing stimuli. They attached the brain cells from a sea lamprey to a small, commercially available robot. Using light, the scientists can stimulate the brain cells to move the robot around. The lamprey ordinarily uses this mechanism for balance - to keep itself centered and upright in the water. As a result, the animal's brain will seek equilibrium, and in most cases the robot will turn to the light and run toward it.

"Rocket Man" Builds Backyard Spaceship

BEND, Oregon - 44-year-old Brian Walker never finished school. In fact, he dropped out after two semesters of engineering college. But this fact is not keeping him from building a rocket in his back yard. The self-made millionaire has already invested $250,000 in his project. The thrust will be produced by a combination of steam and hydrogen peroxide engines. If all goes as planned, his rocket will take him up to 32 miles, where he will experience several moments of weightlessness and then begin to fall back toward Earth. "My whole mission is to show what a person can do on his own," says Walker. "If I die, I die. I'd rather die trying this than spend the next 40 years bitter that I never made the attempt."

L.A. Assessor Boldly Goes Where No Tax Collector Has Gone Before

SACRAMENTO, California - County officials in Los Angeles have set their sights on plans that are truly out of this world. Los Angeles County Assessor Rick Auerbach is reportedly trying to impose property taxes on several satellites that are hovering approximately 22,300 miles above the equator. The $100 million satellites, which are owned by the Los Angeles County-based company Hughes Electronics, are expected to bring in millions of dollars a year in taxes. The idea has apparently sparked a debate "more cosmic than most in the annals of property taxation." But according to Auerbach, "satellites are no different from other movable personal property that he has authority to tax - like boats or construction equipment."

Mind Control Foiled By Aluminum Beanie

All of the victims of cranium invasion can finally put their minds at ease. A non-commercial Internet site has devoted its time and effort to developing a beanie that can stop a person from having his or her brain invaded. The product is an Aluminum Foil Deflector Beanie (AFDB), which reportedly is a type of headgear that can shield your brain from most electro-magnetic psychotronic mind-control carriers. The site provides plans and photographs on how to make a beanie, entirely from foil, that wards off mind-control signals.

Science on the Brink of Eliminating Need for Women

JAPAN - Researchers, feverishly working on the infant science of cloning, believe they have discovered a way to reprogram male reproductive cells into producing eggs. Japanese scientists have been attempting to clone only the seed for a new baby instead of the baby itself. The incredible byproduct of this research is a technique to alter the sexual characteristics of human chromosomes. If successful, men can be both father and mother of children.
[It seems science has finally caught up with Alabama where folks have been father and brother to their children for generations.]

Better Than the Heimlich Maneuver

NORTHERN JAPAN - This could be a new marketing technique for Hoover. A 70-year-old Japanese man choking on a sticky rice cake was saved when his daughter sucked the glob out with a vacuum cleaner. The man from northern Japan suddenly began gasping for air as he chewed on a piece of mochi rice cake, a food traditionally eaten by the Japanese around New Year. Family members first tried unsuccessfully to remove the food with their fingers. Then the man's 46-year-old daughter grabbed a vacuum cleaner, took out his dentures and stuck the hose into his mouth with the switch turned to high. The gooey white mess reportedly emerged and the man was said to have had almost fully recovered by the time paramedics arrived.

Environmentalists Weed out Problems for Hemp Car

A hemp-fueled car scheduled to begin a record-breaking 10,000 mile trip around North America was unveiled in Washington, D.C., at a conference devoted primarily to legalizing marijuana. The car is a white, modified 1983 Mercedes diesel station wagon festooned with colorful hemp-related logos and bearing the license plate "HEMPCAR." It's the creation of Grayson and Kellie Sigler, who plan to use roughly 400 gallons of hemp biodiesel during their trip. Environmentalists say biodiesel fuel is much cleaner than gasoline, putting out 80 percent less emissions than gas. The only distinctive side effect bystanders may experience from the car is a funky odor. Most people who are familiar with the smell of burning marijuana seeds will recognize it.

[The trip may be prolonged due to frequent stops for snacks.]

I'll Take Michael Douglas's Chin to Go, Please

CALIFORNIA - To increase their credibility, stature, and power, American men are increasingly seeking chin implants. According to doctors, a strong chin has become synonymous with status, and those with "weak" chins are perceived as having similar character. Many men think the $2,500 surgery will help save their careers, and the procedure only takes a few hours. In fact, the patients can resume normal activity the next day. Brent Moellken, a Californian plastic surgeon, says that Michael Douglas's chin is the most requested, but it used to be stars like Cary Grant and Clark Gable. Moellken maintains that he knew a television anchorperson whose career soared after having a chin implant.

[I'm almost afraid to ask what could possibly be next...]

Explosive Kitty Litter Sparks Panic in Ohio City

PORTLAND, Ohio - An "atomic kitten" sounds like a character from a new video game, but for people in Portland it was way too real. Radioactive cat urine, that was later traced to a pet cat that was treated for a thyroid tumor with the radioactive substance iodine-131, sparked a safety scare at a nuclear power station. The affected cat litter was among 20 tons of household rubbish found to have dangerous radiation levels. The rubbish was sent to Indian Point nuclear power station in New York state for special handling after setting off alarms. This incident probably could have been diverted had the pet's owners used the special radiation-proof cat litter that can be flushed away.

But Can He Walk and Chew Gum at the Same Time?

BASIRHAT, West Bengal - And I thought that people who are ambidextrous were talented. Indian performer Tapan Dey, 25, can reportedly write with all four limbs in different languages at the same time. Dey writes in Hindi, Assamese, English and Bangla, in front of street audiences and claims he wants to "redefine" the art of calligraphy. "I was inspired when I saw a young boy in Calcutta writing with both hands. I thought I could do better," Dey told reporters. He admitted that there really isn't a future for his "talent" as a profession and would like to become a teacher.

Preemie Baby Truly Proves Good Things Come in Small Packages

OAK LAWN, Illinois - An infant who was no bigger than a can of soda when she entered the world spent her first full day out of the hospital recently. Mia Medina tipped the scales at just 1 pound 1 ounce when she was born March 13, 2001, 18 weeks premature, at Advocate Christ Medical Center in Oak Lawn, Illinois. She had not been expected to live. But doctors put Mia on a respirator and fed her intravenously. Her parents were unable to hold her until she was two months old. "She's got a strong will," her father, Ric Medina, told reporters. Mia is not the smallest baby to survive. The Guinness Book of World Records cites a 10-ounce baby born at 18 weeks in 1989 at Loyola University Medical Center in Maywood, Illinois.

Brit Takes Cow Tipping To The Next Level

SHROPSHIRE, England - You may have heard of potato guns and pumpkin launchers, but have you heard of carcass catapults? A man has been criticized by the RSPCA for hurling dead animals using a 60-foot-high sling made from pine trunks. Huw Kennedy is known worldwide for his reconstruction of medieval siege engines. He usually uses these devices to throw derelict cars and old pianos, but has recently moved on to flinging dead horses, cows and pigs. Apparently this carcass flinging draws quite a crowd. According to Kennedy, "Not all of them burst on impact, but when they do, the local kids love paddling in the guts." An RSPCA spokesman rebutted Kennedy's remarks saying, "This kind of thing hardly promotes a responsible attitude to animals and implies they are disposable for entertainment."

Too Many Bean Bags Produce Fart Bags?

MEXICO - Now you can't drink the water or play with certain toys in Mexico. The Federal Attorney General's Office for Consumers banned sales of so-called Fart Bags and Fragrant Bombs after discovering that they are making kids sick. The toys reportedly produce a farting sound and a putrid odor when sat upon. The nation's health secretariat issued a warning that the citric acid and bicarbonate of soda inside the toys were causing dizziness and vomiting. An estimated total of 5,000 were confiscated over the past weekend.

3

Natural Deselection

In the first edition of The Best of Bizarre News, I included a chapter entitled "Genius...Not!" about some of the stupidest people ever to make it into the newsletter. It proved to be the most popular chapter in the book, perhaps because we have all, at one point in our lives, done things that defy any interpretation of common sense. In the following pages I have collected yet another assortment of apparent nut jobs, many of whom have removed themselves from the gene pool, and several who still have a good chance of doing so. If you read anything in this chapter and say to yourself, "That sounds like it might have been a good idea," then we'll be seeing you in an issue of Bizarre News soon.

Man Shoots Craps While Playing Russian Roulette

HOUSTON, Texas - A 19-year-old Houston boy gambled and lost big time when he decided to play Russian roulette with a .45-caliber semiautomatic pistol. The young man was visiting friends when he announced his intention to play the deadly game. He apparently did not realize that a semiautomatic, unlike a revolver, automatically inserts a cartridge into the firing chamber when the gun is cocked. He apparently lost the game, and his life, all in one shot.

Man Turns to Suicide After Amputation: Survives

BETHLEHEM, Pennsylvania - Those nasty workplace amputations can really hurt. Just ask 25-year-old William Bartron. Last week Bartron cut his hand off while working with a miter saw in a friend's basement. Apparently the pain was so terrible that he tried to end his torment with a pneumatic nail gun. When he was finally found, Bartron had at least a dozen one-inch nails protruding from his head. Miraculously he survived. He underwent emergency surgery to reattach the hand and was last reported in stable condition.

Funeral Director Gets Live One In The Sack

ASHLAND, Massachusetts - Emergency technicians found the body of a 39-year-old woman slumped in a bathtub next to an empty bottle of sleeping pills and assumed she was dead. The funeral director who received the body, John Matarese, agreed. He revised his assessment when he heard gurgling noises coming from the bag. "It scared me half to death," he said. "The girl was alive." Police and emergency technicians were unable to detect any signs of life when they found the woman three-and-a-half hours earlier. She apparently overdosed on pills, police said. The state Department of Public Health is investigating to determine whether emergency workers acted properly.

Man Kills Himself in Ultimate Face-Off

JAY COUNTY, Indiana - A 19-year-old Indiana man entered a "Face-Off" with a loaded firearm and lost. After having apparent trouble firing the gun, Gregory David Pryor decided to look down the barrel to find the source of the problem. Apparently it was just a user error, because the gun fired and shot him in the face.

Man Becomes Butt of a Bad Practical Joke

WOODBINE, New Jersey - A man became the "butt" of a practical joke after being shot to death during a party at his home. Anthony Saduk Jr., 29, and his roommate, Wesley Geisinger, 31, were reportedly hosting a party at their home when Saduk loaded a muzzleloader rifle with cigarette butts and paper towel wadding. Saduk aimed and fired the rifle at Geisinger, who was standing nearby, and he was hit in the chest. Geisinger collapsed and was pronounced dead at the scene. Autopsy reports show that three cigarette butts had penetrated his rib cage directly above his heart, causing his death. Saduk has been charged with aggravated manslaughter, in addition to two counts of aggravated assault in connection with another incident at the party where he shot at Geisinger and Joseph Johnson, 32, with a .44-caliber muzzleloader pistol loaded with gunpowder and tissue paper.

Russian Woman Blows Chance For Breakfast in Bed

RUSSIA - A 30-year-old Russian couple will think twice from now on before having "sausage" with their pancakes. The woman was evidentially performing oral sex on her boyfriend while he was frying pancakes in their kitchen. The tragedy occurred when he dropped the cast-iron pan on her head. The intense pain caused her to involuntarily grit her teeth. As a result, the man is being treated for severe bite wounds on his penis, while his partner suffered a concussion.

First Prize Boozer Falls Head Over Heals

NORWOOD, Ohio - Who would have thunk you can get drunk at an "all-you-can-drink" competition? Apparently not 67-year-old John Remley. He reportedly got so drunk on his free booze prize that staff at Lieb's Cafe moved him away from the bar and allegedly left him unattended near some steps. He then proceeded to fall down the steps, hit his head and was knocked unconscious. Remley is now seeking $1 million in punitive damages, an additional undetermined amount of money for past and future medical bills, and pain and suffering from bar owner Ron Janus for continuing to supply him with alcohol.

Man Mauled While Using Litter Box

BEIJING, China - A group of Bengal tigers were not happy when their keeper tried to use their "litter box." Xu Xiaodong, 19, appears to have climbed the railings of the Bengal tiger cage and pulled his trousers down. Evidence at the scene of the death at the Jinan animal park included toilet paper, excrement and a trouser belt. Zoo officials found the young man's blood-soaked body lying on the ground surrounded by tigers. Police believe Xu climbed the wall of a partially-constructed building used to raise the tigers to relieve himself. They said the smell probably caused the tigers to pounce.

Cigarette + Gas = Explosion

BRISBANE, Australia - Common sense tells us that gasoline is a volatile substance and should be kept away from an open flame. However, a 40-year-old drunken Australian man must have been lacking in that department for he blew himself in the air after lighting a cigarette while filling a gas can. The petrol exploded, his car burst into flames and the man was blown 15 feet through the air. To add insult to injury, he then came crashing to earth on a nest of angry ants.

According to the police, the man only suffered minor burns and did not require hospital treatment. He was later charged with drunk-driving, driving without a license and driving an unregistered vehicle.

Death By Train or Snake?

NORIAS, Texas - Where is the best place to sleep outdoors in Texas? One would think it would not be actually "on" a set of train tracks, but apparently several illegal aliens and homeless people had that exact idea. The belief is that poisonous snakes will not cross over the tracks. Six alleged illegal aliens were hiding from the reptiles one night when a freight train passed through the area. Spokeswoman for the Border Control Letty Garza said, "The train crew saw some debris on the tracks. The next split-second they saw heads raise up, and then six people were killed instantly." On the plus side, no snake bites were discovered on the bodies.

Missouri Man Bakes Fireworks, Blows Up Kitchen

KANSAS CITY, Missouri - Fireworks hidden in a Kansas City man's oven turned out to be a recipe for disaster when the man blew up his oven during dinner preparations. According to Kansas City Assistant Fire Marshall Jim Duddy, the explosion occurred early on the morning of the Fourth of July at the home of a 28-year-old man who had spent the night celebrating with friends. The group, "who had been drinking heavily," were shooting fireworks off for several hours on Tuesday night at the Northland area home. Neighbors became annoyed with the noise and called the police. When they arrived, someone in the group stashed the fireworks in the oven but neglected to inform the homeowner that they were there. Later, when he turned on the oven to bake lasagna at 3:00 a.m., the kitchen was blown to smithereens. Duddy concluded that flying glass had caused some injuries, but otherwise no one was hurt.

Coffin Maker Puts Penis a Cut Above the Rest

MOSCOW - A coffin maker almost laid his penis to rest for good after his trousers got caught in his circular saw. The mangled appendage was sawed into six pieces and the agonized man was rushed to a special clinic that only treats injuries to the male genitals. The Emergency Care for Men was established at a Moscow hospital in 1999. Professor Pyotr Shcheplev set up the department to develop the field of andrology, which focuses on the study of the male genitals. Dr. Shcheplev summed up his mission by stating, "If a penis has some defect, it is a big psychological blow. It's a man's dignity." [Dr. Shcheplev, men everywhere "salute" you!]

Hocus Pocus 'Spells' Death For Ghana Man

GHANA - Perhaps a twenty-three-year old Ghana man should have asked for an intelligence spell instead. Aleobiga Aberima was reportedly shot dead by a fellow villager while testing a magic spell designed by a witch doctor to make him bulletproof. After smearing his body with a concoction of herbs every day for two weeks, Aberima volunteered to be shot to check if the spell had worked. Aberima died instantly from a single bullet. After the shooting, villagers began to beat the witch doctor severely until a village elder rescued him.

Woman Gets Burnt Bottom From Lover's Afterglow

BALCESTI, Romania - A Romanian Woman received a burnt bottom from the "afterglow" of her boyfriend's post-sex cigarette. Alina Munteanu's boyfriend started a forest fire by throwing his cigarette butt out of his car window. As the flames rose, Alina and her lover jumped out naked and tried to fight the fire with a blanket. Unfortunately, the 21-year-old burnt her bottom in the process and was later taken to a local hospital after firefighters were dispatched to put out the flames.

Man Stiches Mouth Shut in Protest

GOTEBORG, Sweden - A 35-year-old Swedish inmate appealed his three-year sentence for a narcotics violation, but the reduction request was denied. In protest, the man stitched his lips together last week and has not eaten since. How this could possibly help his case we really aren't sure. How did a criminal even have access to a needle and thread? According to Uno Rodin, head of the prison, "Needles have never been considered a safety problem, and nobody had imagined that this could happen." The inmate will further appeal the decision to the Supreme Court.

Couple Injured in Freak Accident

HUNTSVILLE, Alabama - Things definitely heated up in the kitchen for an Alabama couple after they tried to warm up a few aerosol paint cans in their oven. John and Ruby Barnes, from Huntsville, claimed they "were trying to make the paint come out of the can easier." The paint came out easier all right, followed by a ball of flames when they opened the oven door. Ruby Barnes received second-degree burns to 20 percent of her body. Her husband suffered first and second-degree burns on his face, hands and arms. Both are recuperating in the burn unit of the hospital at the University of Alabama in Birmingham.

Man Nails His Head to a Plank

OLDHAM, England - If you thought the man who nailed his leg to the board was bizarre, read this. A 44-year-old warehouse worker from Oldham, England accidentally nailed his head to 15-foot plank. Jimmy McKenzie apparently stood up without realizing there was a six-inch nail in a piece of wood above him and was trapped for an hour while firemen sawed down the plank. Fortunately the nail did not pierce his brain and he was released from the hospital with minor injuries.

The World's Most Unnecessary Protest

CANBERRA, Australia - A 48-year-old Pakistani man was granted permanent residence in Australia several years ago and has been trying to secure visas for his family ever since. Not realizing that his case had been approved, the man lit himself on fire in protest at the entrance to the parliament building in Canberra. A witness said, "He was rolling around on the ground...but he stopped moving by the time anybody went out there with a fire extinguisher." The man was reportedly upset that his family had yet to receive visas, but according to local papers, the protest was unnecessary because the visas had already been okayed. The man remains in critical condition in a burns unit at Sydney's Concord Hospital.

Woman Has Foggiest Idea About Bug Extermination

LOS ANGELES - A woman got zapped during an attempt to exterminate bugs in her home. The woman, whose identity was not immediately released, activated 30 fogger-style "bug bombs" in her home, including one in the kitchen area. Some sort of ignition source triggered an explosion that authorities say burned the woman, shattered the windows and lifted the roof three inches. According to fire spokesman Jim Wells, no more than three or four foggers should have been used and the blast caused about $30,000 damage to the 800-square-foot home.

Getting Nailed Is a Heartbreaker for Tennessee Man

DICKSON, Tennessee - Tennessee maintenance worker Joe Kern really takes his work to heart. The 52-year-old father of ten slipped while using a nail gun to carry out repairs on a trailer. Kern told reporters that the nail was sticking out of his body with an inch of it lodged in the breast bone. He also said he had a good idea it hit the heart because he could feel the heart beat through the nail. Now, instead of going straight to hospital, he wanted to tell his wife Pam what had happened so she "would not come apart." A co-worker drove Kern home before he was air-lifted to Vanderbilt University Medical Center where surgeons removed the nail and repaired a hole in his right ventricle.

A Pain in the Rear Ends Model's Career

MANCHESTER, England - Receiving an injection in her bottom has left a 23-year-old nude model in a pinch. Laura Mackenzie-Hawkins, who works as an art class model, says the jab left her back-side disfigured. According to Mackenzie-Hawkins, modeling agencies are no longer interested because of her scarred bottom and that her prospects of lucrative magazine and calendar work have been ruined. Also, she had attended four more still-life sessions after the scar appeared, but was devastated when she saw it on artists' sketches. "I'm an exhibitionist and I loved my job. Now it's like having a piece missing from me," she concluded.

How Much is Your Penis Worth?

NASHVILLE, Tennessee - In 1998, Arthur C. Tucker Jr. went to Vanderbilt University Medical Center for treatment for a swollen prostate gland. The doctors used the Prostatron system which is used to destroy excess prostate cells with a beam of microwaves, but during Tucker's appointment, something went terribly wrong. Nurses told him that the pain he felt was normal when it turns out the catheter may have slipped during the procedure causing the microwaves to be directed at his penis. His penis was burnt so badly that he stayed in bed for nearly a month, and then the member still had to be amputated. Tucker and his wife sued the hospital and EDAP Technomed Inc., which distributed the device, for $13 million. They reached an out-of-court settlement this week and the couple is reportedly "satisfied."

Man Sets Himself on Fire; Charged with Arson

HONG KONG - To protest his Social Security allotment, 52-year-old Lam Leung-wai set himself on fire at the Social Welfare Department headquarters. Later, while recovering at the hospital, Police charged him with arson. Welfare advocates call the charge inhumane and unreasonable. Police explained that the protestor started a fire on the 24th floor of the building and then purposely leapt into it, thus constituting at least a holding arson charge. A spokesman for the Department of Justice says the charge is not final, though. He explained, "A holding charge means that the police preliminarily find that the man should be charged. But it can only be finalized after consulting us."

Just Call Him Stumpy

BALTIMORE CITY, Maryland - Edward Stamper put his manhood in the hands Dr. David Goldstein when he went for a penile dysfunction operation. Following the surgery, however, Stamper believed his penis had been shortened and sued the doctor. Various complications allegedly followed the surgery, including the webbing of his penile tissues which caused it to pull toward his pelvis thereby cutting the original length in half. A jury in Baltimore City awarded the patient $1 million for the pain and suffering he endured, and perhaps for grief counseling. Wife Oma Gay Stamper received her own sum of $500,000 for the estimated effect on their marriage.

'Honey Monster' Performs Expensive Practical Joke

LONDON, England - It could be considered the ultimate "congealed" weapon- 320 pounds of raw, body fat. Andrew Baldry, who is of the aforementioned weight, performed a belly-flop on 140-pound co-worker Christopher Purvis at the meat packing plant in Beccles, eastern England. Purvis said the 6-foot 2-inch Baldry, nicknamed

"Honey Monster," belly-flopped on top of him as three other workers pinned him down. He suffered cracked ribs and has not returned to work since the incident last June. Judge John Holt of Bury St. Edmunds Crown Court ordered Baldry to perform 180 hours community service and to pay Purvis $1,000.

Previous Owner Reluctant To Leave Old Home

CHICAGO, Illinois - Waking up the neighbors is evidentially not an issue in a small town on Chicago's North Side. The owner of a bungalow in this region apparently died in February 1997. The trouble is, no one noticed until the new owner of the property at 5339 N. Central opened the door and found Adolph Stec still sitting in his living room chair - a newspaper from February 1997 at his side. Ronald Ohr of Glenview, Illinois, purchased the Stec property for back taxes. "It was a pitiful sight," Ohr's wife, Jeanne, told reporters. Neighbors said Stec, born 76 years ago in Poland, was a loner who kept to himself after his companion of 25 years, Brigita Rogucz, died about five years ago. They thought he had abandoned the place.

Getting Nailed Never Felt So Good For Danish Man

DENMARK - One may have heard the expression "hanging by a thread" before, but never by a nail through the leg. Jan Madsen was saved from falling to his eminent death by a nail gun as he worked on his holiday home, near Berlin. The 27-year-old accidentally fired the nail gun, which shot the pneumatically-driven nail all the way through his knee and into the wooden support beams. Madsen remained conscious as emergency crews worked for more than an hour to free him from the roof. He was then rushed to the hospital where doctors operated immediately. They say he will suffer no long-term problems from the accident.

Woman Helps Take a Bite out of Crime

CHICAGO, Illinois - In most self-defense classes, the instructor is likely to tell the students to strike the attacker where it hurts. A 42-year-old Chicago woman took this sentiment one step further. She bit off the testicles of a man who sexually assaulted her and took them to the police headquarters just a short distance away from the attack. Officer Thomas Donegan told reporters, "During the assault, the female victim got the man's testicles in her mouth and bit them off." The attacker went to a local hospital, but reattachment surgery proved futile. The woman was treated at a different facility.

Man Dies from Swallowing Fish

IRON COUNTY, Missouri - It was another rendition of "Stupid Human Tricks" when a drunken Missouri man decided to swallow a live fish and choked to death on it. An inebriated Todd Poller, 45, told his friends to watch him as he grabbed a five-inch perch from a creek. He dropped it headfirst into his mouth, but it lodged in his throat. He began choking and gasping for air. His friends tried to dislodge the fish by using the Heimlich Maneuver, but it was too late. Poller was dead by the time an ambulance arrived. According to Alan Mathes, Sheriff of Iron County, the autopsy report showed Poller died from asphyxiation from having a fish lodged in his throat. In addition to this, he also suffered lacerations to the inside of his throat from the fish's fins.

Man Survives Deep Plunge into Tampa Bay

PINELLAS COUNTY, Florida - An identified man has become the sixth person to have survived a suicide attempt off of the Skyway Bridge over Tampa Bay. After a 200-foot fall into the bay, the man reportedly hit the water with such an impact that his clothing was ripped off. Witnesses say that after his jump he was able to swim about 40 yards to nearby rocks. He told rescuers: "I'm hurt bad!" A member of a St. Petersburg fire department told reporters that it's a miracle he survived the jump. Statistics show that the structure is the third-deadliest bridge for suicides in the country, following the Golden Gate Bridge and San Diego's Coronado Bridge respectively.

Padded Bra Gives Woman 'False' Sense of Security

FRANKENMUTH, Michigan - Bullet-proof vests have been around a while, but have you ever heard of a nail-proof bra? Dana Colwell, 31, was cutting the grass at her Frankenmuth home when a one-and-a-half-inch nail shot out from under the mower and punctured her right breast. Fortunately, she was wearing her Maidenform padded "liquid-curved" bra, which broke the speed of the nail enough so it stopped short of her heart. She told reporters she'll make sure she's wearing the breast-enhancing bra whenever she mows the lawn in the future. I am sure her neighbors will love to know that, too.

Internet 'Hacker's' Plan Is a Cut Above the Rest

BILOXI, Missouri - A partially paralyzed man is hoping to cash in on the fact that prosthetic limbs cost an arm and a leg. Paul Morgan, 33, of Biloxi, Missouri has set up a web site where online viewers can watch him amputate his own feet. This macabre act is part of Morgan's plan to raise enough money for a new set of prosthetic limbs. Morgan, who is unemployed, lost the use of his feet almost 15 years ago when he fell from a moving pickup truck. According to Morgan, Medicare refuses to pay for a set of $200,000 hyrdraulic legs because they are unnecessary. Even if the gruesome proposition doesn't bring in online voyeurs with a taste for the macabre, Morgan says he still plans on going ahead with the procedure on Halloween, October 31st.

Can You Imagine If He Had Dental Floss?

GREAT BRITAIN - A toothbrush was used to relieve a different "cavity" when a pensioner decided to use the dental instrument to scratch his hemorrhoids. The 69-year-old man was ordered into the hospital after the toothbrush became lodged in his rectum. An X-ray revealed it was deep inside near his pelvis. Although this was the first recorded case of a toothbrush having to be removed from a rectum, the British Dental Journal reports doctors have recovered toothbrush holders, toothbrush packages and toothpicks in the past.

Work Not Just a Roll in the Hay for Farmer

ROBBINSDALE, Minnesota - A 34-year-old Minnesota farmer risked life and limb, literally, after he was pulled into a hay baler. Jarrod Wagner was removing a clump of hay from the twin rollers in the machine when his left arm got caught and he felt himself being dragged in. He used a metal piece from his headset as a crude saw to amputate his own arm. Wagner told reporters, "It was kind of sucking my whole body in, so I figured, well, it was either my whole body or my arm." Hospital officials say that the arm was recovered; however, it was too mangled to be reattached. Wagner is in fair condition after the incident.

Contortionist Fails To Get A Leg Up In The World

LONDON, England - Talk about getting wrapped up in your work. Berkine, a Netherlands National Circus performer, reportedly got his right foot stuck on his left shoulder while rehearsing in Gillingham, southeastern England. "I think the problem was that I did not warm up very well," stated the 21-year-old contortionist from Kazakhstan. And according to circus producer Chris Barltrop, Berkine's co-workers ignored him at first because they just thought it was part of the act. They finally noticed he was being serious and came to his aid.

Bizarre Sex Act Leaves Naked Man Hanging

PENCAENEWYDD, North Wales - A Welsh man paid a high price for his fetish when he hung himself in front of his webcam. Tony Rogerson apparently suffocated after tying a dog leash around his neck and hanging himself from a roof beam. He had been chatting on the Net with a stranger named "Guy 27" and filming himself with a webcam. Seconds before Rogerson died he typed out the message: "If you want to see me hang, say 'yes.'" He was later found hanging naked by his 14-year-old son.

Man Performs His Own Castration

SASKATCHEWAN, Canada - There is a saying that goes "desperate times lead to desperate measures," but this is a little ridiculous. A 28-year-old man from Alberta wanted to have his testicles removed immediately because he felt "the testosterone was poisoning his body." He found a website on the Internet about human castration that was hosted by former chef Gary Gillingwater, who claims he learned all about the procedure by practicing on farm animals as a child. The two men met in a hotel room in Fort Qu'Appelle, Saskatchewan, where Gillingwater carried out the procedure without the use of anesthetics. Gillingwater pleaded guilty to causing bodily harm before a provincial count and received an 18-month suspended sentence and was ordered to perform community service.

4

You Have the Right to Remain Silent

It has been said that crime does not pay, unless of course you're trying to sell Bizarre News books. Criminals and their stories have always been an invaluable addition to Bizarre News, and the following chapter is a tribute to their inadvertent talent for entertainment. Whether it's the bank robber who dropped his resume at the scene of the crime, the thieves who stopped in the middle of a get-away for a cup of coffee or the mystery attacker who sneaks up on women and licks their feet, bizarre criminals will always have a home here.

Man Severs Penis in Bizarre Religious Movement

SAO PAULO - In order to "bring himself closer to God," a 23-year-old convicted Brazilian rapist sliced off his own penis and flushed it down the toilet. Flavio dos Santos Cruz was found by prison guards screaming and bleeding in his cell. "It is written in Bible that if a part of your body distances you from God and makes you commit a sin, you should cut it off," Cruz told reporters. According to urologist Aerton Barbosa Neves, who operated on Cruz, he will now have to urinate through a tube, but can still impregnate someone, "albeit only with medical assistance."

Stealing Jewelry Was Easy to Stomach for Thief

Police are anxiously awaiting the arrival of a "shipment" of stolen jewelry from the thief that stole it. The suspect was found lying injured in the street with a broken hip after jumping from a window with a bag of jewelry. In a fit of panic, he swallowed the evidence. An X-ray of the man's hip revealed the stolen merchandise nestled away in his stomach. Police are now guarding him around the clock to make sure they can retrieve the jewelry as soon as "nature takes its course."

Girls Unimpressed - Koala Doesn't Fit on Finger

SAN FRANCISCO - Authorities have arrested two teenagers for stealing a pair of koalas from the San Francisco Zoo. What would a couple of young kids want with the expensive, exotic and hard-to-care-for animals? Not to sell them for a profit, but to show them off to their girlfriends. Zoo officials said the thieves appeared to have broken through a skylight and slipped into the koala exhibit. It was unreported whether the stunt had the desired effect on the girlfriends. The teens, however, were much impressed with the charges of burglary, possession of stolen property, and grand theft.

A Successful Getaway Was Only A Clicker Away

Two burglars would have gotten away with their haul of televisions if it weren't for one factor. As the pair were about to speed off, they realized they had forgotten the remote controls, so they returned to get them. By then, a resident had already alerted police after she'd spotted the two men outside her neighbor's house loading a television into a sport utility vehicle. Police said they found Jaron Grosby, 20, behind the wheel of the SUV, and Wesley Jackson, 20, hiding behind the vehicle. Jackson reportedly confessed to the officers that he and Grosby stole the televisions after breaking a window to get into the house.

Scam Costs Unsuspecting Puppies a Paw and a Leg

OSAKA, Japan - A 63-year-old Japanese man was arrested for operating a scam that literally cost puppies a paw and a leg. The man is alleged to have sawed off the right front leg of a three-month-old female Dalmatian in late November and the legs of more than ten other puppies since December, 1999. After the mutilation takes place, he is said to have begged for donations from the public in Osaka for the dogs treatment, using a sign reading: "Please donate money because my dog was hit by a car." The man reportedly faces charges for violating the Law Concerning the Protection and Control of Animals and may be sentenced for one year in prison or a large fine.

Mugger Makes A Spectacle With Eyeglass Fetish

A mugger could have been suffering from "optical delusions" that stolen glasses made him better in bed. Police arrested the man after he mugged a stranger on the street and stole his spectacles. According to his wife, he could only become aroused when he wore a freshly-stolen pair of glasses. She says he would return from walks with a pair of stolen glasses and insist she wore her usual pair. Police reportedly found more than 50 pairs of expensive designer glasses in his flat.

Smuggler Swallows Wad of Cash

COLOMBIA - A wad of dough was obviously not too hard for a Colombian man to swallow. Alejandro Londono, 25, was arrested for money laundering at an airport in the western city of Pereira after allegedly swallowing $40,000 and trying to smuggle it into the country. Apparently Londono packed the cash inside fingers cut from latex surgical gloves, each of which contained notes of eight denominations, and swallowed them.

Man Steals $82,000 One Kilowatt At a Time

A 91-year-old Utah man, who authorities said drew free electricity from a nearby power line for decades, finally faces theft charges. Clarence Stucki is charged with stealing about $82,000 worth of power. But officials from Logan Light and Power said Stucki admitted tapping into the line as early as World War II, so the total is likely much higher. The statute of limitations, however, prevents Stucki from being charged what the power company considers the full amount. The old crook would still be getting away with it if he hadn't called his local utility to complain about an outage. Crews correcting the problem discovered the diverted connection on the roof.

Robber Exchanges Hostage for Chicken Sandwich

MILWAUKEE, Wisconsin - Only in Wisconsin would a robber give up a hostage in exchange for a chicken sandwich and a soda. A knife-wielding robber stormed into a Milwaukee shop and grabbed a young woman, threatening bodily harm unless staff members handed over some cash. The robber revealed during negotiations with shop worker Jaspal Singh that he was hungry. Singh gave the would-be robber a sandwich and a can of pop in exchange for the girl while discretely dialing the police. The robber ate until the police arrived to arrest him.

The Not So Great Escape

DEVIZES, England - What seemed like a lucky break proved to be detrimental to Erlestoke prisoners Robert Denvey, Frank Riorden and Samuel Kerrigan. The trio escaped the penitentiary via a ladder they found conveniently propped against a prison wall and a car they found on the other side with its engine running. However, the eyes of fate were not smiling upon them and the trio crashed the car into a ditch in thick fog just a few miles from the prison. Too embarrassed to turn back, they handed themselves over to a woman out walking and asked her to call the police. This little excursion has added an extra 15 months jail time to each man's sentence.

Arsonist Gets Burned By Boasting About Fiery Deed

HAMBURG, New York - It is generally not a good idea to call a fire chief if you're an arsonist and have just started a fire. Nichols Breidenstein did just that after allegedly setting fire to a shop in Hamburg, New York. After the deed he tried to call a friend to boast about it, but accidentally dialed local fire chief Michael Guadango instead. According to Guadango he heard Breidenstein say, "Dude, it's lit. The whole corner's going." It wasn't until then that he realized had just incriminated himself and is now facing arson charges.

Wedding Reception Bites for Bridegroom

NEW ZEALAND - This sounds like it should have happened in Alabama. During the reception, a guest at a wedding bit the bridegroom's scrotum during an argument between the man and the bride's sister. The brawl escalated even further when the groom's brother was kicked in the head, an injury which left him concussed, suffering memory loss and needing five stitches to his jaw. The unruly guest was later charged with two counts of assault and possession of a knife.

Woman Believes Cure For AIDS Is No Bull

CAMBODIA - A 47-year-old woman has been arrested in Phnom Penh, the capital of Cambodia, for allegedly selling cow dung as a cure-all for many illnesses such as A.I.D.S. According to police, the woman instructed consumers on how to apply the product. The muck would cure the various illnesses if the person mixed it with water and then either drank it or sprinkled it on his or her body. Local journalist Rasmei Kampuchea has further information. One Cambodian legend relates an instance when the spirits of two brothers took the form of a person and a cow. According to Kampuchea, the woman claims she and the "sacred cow" were possessed in this manner. And that's no bull.

Man Blames Drunk-Driving On Fire-Eating Class

CALIFORNIA - A California resident has come up with a legitimate reason to test above the legal alcohol limit for drunk driving. When police officers pulled over magician Randall Richman, they claim his eyes were bloodshot, he could barely stand, smelled of alcohol and neglected to carry his license. A breath test estimated Richman's alcohol level to be twice the legal limit, but the magician maintains that he had been teaching a fire-eating class in Hollywood just prior to being stopped. The case will go to court on April 12, when the 32-year-old will contest the breath test. Richman will argue that there were three types of lighter fluid detected, not alcohol. Perhaps by April, Richman will come up with an explanation for the bloodshot eyes...

Man Charged With De-Stiffing Stiff

CALIFORNIA - Sometimes you really have to wonder what goes through these people's minds. Tommy Laws from Fresno, California, is to be tried on charges of mutilation of a corpse after he cut the penis off the body of John Sheehan and stuck it in a jar. Laws's friend,

Roland Thomas, has been charged with murder, accused of shooting the businessman after hitting him over the head with a whisky bottle. Laws allegedly used a kitchen knife to hack off the dead man's penis, kept it overnight and then flushed it away in a motel toilet. A judge at Fresno County Superior Court has ruled there is enough evidence to try the case after Thomas's girlfriend pleaded guilty to charges including "accessory after the fact".

Man Confuses 911 with 976

NEW YORK - A 22-year-old New York man allegedly called the Colonie City police station five times hoping to hire a companion for the night. The man supposedly confused the police department phone number with an ad in a personals column. After he called back the fifth time, the female operator decided to let the man fulfill his wishes. The two agreed to meet at a hotel, but when the suspect got there, police were waiting and arrested him for soliciting sex. One would think the man would comprehend that it was not an escort service when the woman answered "Colonie Police Department, how may I help you?

Robbers Take Note: Don't Give Them Your Name

SAN FRANCISCO, California - The allegedly drunk Scot Alan Beane, 37, set a new standard for criminals when he left a resume and receipt with his name on it at a bank he robbed. Police officers found Beane because the resume listed his previous address, and he has since been charged with robbing four banks totaling over $13,000. He originally left a Western Union money-transfer receipt with his name on it at one bank in March, but his luck ran out during the following bank robbery when he actually left his resume behind. San Francisco police Lt. Bruce Marovich told the Chronicle, "Here's the story - you shouldn't drink or take drugs and drive. You shouldn't rob banks and do the same thing. That's what he was doing."

Human Flesh for Sale Just Around the Corner

CHISINAU, Moldova - Everyone knows that all meat is not of the same freshness and quality, but imagine if the meat you purchased for Sunday dinner turned out to be human flesh. Police have arrested two women in the former Soviet Republic of Moldova for selling human flesh outside a butcher's shop. Tests confirmed that the supposed meat was indeed human flesh, and the two were officially charged with selling outlawed meat. In order to avoid public panic, police waited until the test results were announced to give a statement about the arrest.

Robber Tries to Confess, But No One Listens

NEW ORLEANS, Louisiana - Ricardo Antonio Pacheco, a bank vault manager at Bank One, had been stealing from the institution since 1991. Guilt-ridden for taking $663,000, he resigned on March 8th and immediately tried to confess to federal prosecutors. Vinny Mosca, Pacheco's lawyer, said, "What makes this so bizarre is that there was never even a suspicion, not even a hint. He used a complex record-keeping system to keep this thing going. He survived an audit every month." When Pacheco tried to give his story, the U.S. attorney's office declined an appointment until the following week because they were just too busy. If the government does not want to hear about your transgressions, shouldn't you be able to just keep the money?

Judge Orders Man To Keep It In His Pants

WISCONSIN - The Wisconsin Supreme Court will soon hear arguments on whether a deadbeat dad's constitutional rights were violated by a judge's order prohibiting him from fathering any more children until he can prove he's supporting the nine he already has. David Oakley, 34, was sentenced to three years in prison for failing to pay

$25,000 in child support, and the judge also imposed a five year probation during which he cannot father any more children. Oakley's ex-wife and mother of four has little sympathy for him. "All he does is get women pregnant all the time and then not pay child support."

Pathetic Prankster Pilfers Plus-sized Panties

LONG ISLAND, New York - Being shy is one thing, but this is bordering on pathetic. A 44-year-old New York man has been charged with stealing credit card numbers so he could buy undies over the phone while flirting with the operators. According to shy guy Scott Hanko, he was too shy to pick up a phone and talk to a woman normally, so he felt compelled to order plus-sized underwear and engage in male-female banter with the operator. Hanko is accused of using 1,200 credit card numbers and ordering thousands of dollars worth of extra-large lingerie, which were sent to the unsuspecting card owners over ten years. The case only surfaced when catalogue company JC Penney noticed they were having a lot of large-sized underwear returned to them.

Man Sells His Urine for Drug Tests

HENDERSONVILLE, North Carolina - In the great spirit of American entrepreneurship, Kenneth Curtis created a website called Privacy Protection Services. To combat routine work drug tests, the owner sells his own urine in kits including heat packets for the consumer to warm the urine to body temperature. The sample comes in a pouch supplied with tubing to be taped to the body. The Service also claims that if used properly, the item can be undetected by those supervising the test. The court system, however, did not appreciate Curtis's service, and he was recently arrested. Disagreeing with the charge, he told CNews: "If you can't sell urine, what can you sell? I don't sell drugs, I sell urine."
[He's got a point there.]

Policeman Marks Girl For Sex

TAIPEI - It could be the considered the "Scarlet Letter" of the new millennium. Officer Feng Te-Ming has allegedly branded a schoolgirl on the breast with the words "night cat," which is slang for prostitute. The two supposedly got together after meeting on the Internet. Te-Ming took the 17-year-old girl to his home and accused her of being a prostitute after she took a mobile phone call. Investigators say the officer and the girl agreed to the branding with a heated steel wire as punishment if he agreed not to arrest her. Te-Ming has since been fired and has paid compensation to the girl.

Mother Turns Her 7-Year-Old In To Cops

BISMARCK, North Dakota - When a mother in Bismarck realized she was missing money from a stash left on her kitchen counter, she immediately questioned her two sons. The seven-year-old fessed up to his crime: he stole $6 for a Beanie Baby. By way of punishment, the mother turned her son in to the authorities. Police Lt. Nick Sevart said, "She wanted him cited for theft, so that is what we did." The boy received a criminal citation and was released to his mother. The case will wind up in juvenile court. Sevart explained, "The reason we determine consequences is to help them avoid this type of trouble in the future."
[This way the boy will be completely familiar with the criminal system by the time he starts hot-wiring cars.]

Thief Tells Police on Himself

HELSINGBORG, Sweden - A 20-year-old man developed what he thought to be a fool-proof robbery plan. He would wait for the home and garden store employees to leave for the night and take merchandise. All was going according to plan as he stuffed items in a duvet cover, when he realized he had no way out of the store. He tried opening the front door with a crowbar and attempted to break through a wall in the restrooms. Both efforts were to no avail. He finally gave up and called the police for help. The authorities were too happy to bail him out and promptly arrest him.

Bizarre Burglaries Have Brits Baffled

MANCHESTER, England - Many thieves will go after scores of cash, others will go for expensive jewelry or flashy cars. But thieves in Manchester, England, apparently have a different agenda. In one case, intruders smashed a high-tech security system at a biscuit factory to steal a small monetary value of wafers. In another, burglars stole thousand of dollars worth of motorcycles and the shop's pet cockatoo. David Evans, of Gorton-based Two Cities Insurance Services, stated: "We have had more theft claims in the last month than in the past five years, yet there is no logic to the kinds of shops targeted."

Alleged Robber Refuses Surgery and Is Acquitted

PHILADELPHIA, Pennsylvania - A masked man on a bicycle shot at two men during a robbery last August in Philadelphia. The robber fled after being shot by one of the victims. When 18-year-old Nathan Pailin went to the hospital the same night for a gunshot wound, police began investigating him. Though his wound was treated, doctors were unable to remove all the fragments. Now there is a court order to have the remains removed from Pailin's chest to see if the bullet matches the one from the crime scene. Pailin's attorney, however, claims the court order is a violation of her client's constitutional rights against unlawful search and seizure. Since the suspect refuses to have surgery, and with no other evidence available, Judge Pamela Pryor Dembe acquitted Pailin of robbery, aggravated assault and a weapons charge.

My Addiction Made Me Do It!

CHICAGO, Illinois - In what is believed to be a precedent-setting ruling, a judge reduced a Chicago woman's sentence because of a shopping addiction. Elizabeth Roach stole almost a quarter of a million dollars from a past employer and claimed she went on spending sprees because she is a shopaholic. Instead of the maximum 18-month jail term, Judge Matthew Kennelly gave her five years probation. Additionally, she is prohibited from getting any credit cards or incurring any new debt. Roach stole $241,061 over the course of three years. Believing her addiction is the source of her problems, the judge did not want a prison term to interrupt her therapy and chance of recovery. He fined her $30,000.

Following Daddy's Footsteps

AUSTIN, Texas - A scant two weeks after President Bush's 19-year-old daughter Jenna was cited for underage drinking, she and her twin sister Barbara were caught trying to buy alcohol at Chuy's, a popular Austin restaurant famous for its margaritas. When asked for identification in her own home town, the daughter of the leader of the free world produced someone else's driver's license. Restaurant employees confiscated the ID and the manager called the police. This will be a second offense for Jenna and a first for Barbara. The restaurant apologized to the first family for having to blow the whistle on the twins.

Flatulent Officer Busted for Breaking Code of Silence

LONDON - A British Officer is getting charged with assault with a "deadly" weapon after allegedly breaking wind during a drug raid and failing to apologize. A Scotland Yard spokesman confirmed that the Department of Professional Standards was investigating a charge that an officer broke wind in the complainants' hallway during a drug raid but did not apologize to the homeowners. The homeowners complained because they felt that the officer's actions were "rude and unprofessional." Police did not confirm what discipline the officer might receive if found guilty of breaking wind.

Prisoners Freed Because of False Fax

AJACCIO, France - Prison officials quickly complied when they received a fax from the magistrate instructing them to free three French prisoners. The prisoners were investigated for illegal possession of firearms and attempted extortion, and the fax demanding their release turned out to be fake. The prison officials, however, did not doubt the document because it was written on official stationery, so they neglected to check the originating fax number or followup with the judge for confirmation. The prisoners' supposed "release" is now a successful escape.

Prisoner Jumps Out of Frying Pan and Into the Fire

SAN JOSE, California - An inmate at Elmwood Correctional Facility should have planned his escape route a little more carefully. Arnold Ancheta, 25, broke out of a medium-security dorm only to hop the wrong fence and end up next door at the women's jail. According to Mark Cursi, a Department of Corrections spokesman, Ancheta apparently escaped by squeezing through the bar on the roof of his cell and breaking out the Plexiglas-covered skylight. He jumped down about 20 feet from the roof. However, instead of heading toward the fence that leads to a public road, he jumped a smaller fence and ended up on the women's side of the facility. Female inmates saw Ancheta running around the yard and told correctional officers. He was taken to a hospital and then to a downtown jail.

Robber Gets Busted for Drug-Induced Cat Nap

AHMAN, Jordan - A jittery robber became a little too relaxed after taking sleeping tablets to calm his nerves during a raid on a hospital pharmacy. The thief managed to slip into the pharmacy through the cooling system, which was undergoing maintenance work. He proceeded to take three tablets from the haul of medication he had stolen and promptly fell asleep while still on the premises. He was found by hospital employees who alerted police.

Swiss Police Find Stash of Suits on Thick-legged Men

ZURICH, Switzerland - Police officers became suspicious when they saw three men with immensely thick legs having difficulty walking out of a retail store. The officers stopped the suspects and discovered full suits wrapped around their legs. Officers indicated the trousers and jackets were folded just so in order to wrap nicely around the limbs. Police also reported a hoard of fashionable men's suits in the boot of their rental car.

'Chalupa' Criminal Charges Cops

FORT WORTH, Texas - Now here's a Taco Bell promotion in the making. Lakount Maddox, 17, allegedly tried to hold up a Taco Bell restaurant shortly after midnight. Employees claim the young man was riding a bicycle when he apparently brandished a gun and demanded the cash in the register. He also ordered a chalupa to go. What he didn't know was while one restaurant worker prepared his meal, another employee was calling 911. When the police arrived, Maddox was still waiting outside the window for his food. He then charged at the officers on his bicycle and waved what was later identified as a toy pellet gun at them. He was shot twice, once in the arm and once in the leg, and was taken to a local hospital where he was listed in good condition.

Stand Off at 200 Feet Lasts 17 Hours

ATLANTA, Georgia - Michael Kelly, 23, put on his best suit and climbed up a 200-foot construction crane last week to hold police and rescuers off for over 17 hours. He spent the day reading a Bible, scribbling notes and, at one point, dropping a blank check into the crowd gathered below. After psychologists failed to talk him down, police threw reason to the wind and called Kelly's mother. She also failed to persuade him to surrender. Early on, police feared that the man had a gun and evacuated about 250 workers from the construction site. The reason for the stand-off was not known.

Drunken Church Burglar Has Much to Wine About

SOROCABA, Brazil - A church burglar in Brazil received no redemption after he got drunk on two bottles of Holy Communion wine. Francimar Pereira Lira, 22, allegedly stole money, a hoover and a camera from the church of Sorocaba, Brazil, before "looking for some refreshment" from the wine. The local priest, Camilo Joao Munaro, found Lira asleep in one of the pews and turned him over to the authorities.

Police Remain One Step Behind Mystery Attacker

PITTSBURGH, Pennsylvania - It appears that a mystery attacker in Pittsburgh may have had some sort of foot fetish after he stopped a woman on the street to sniff her shoe and lick her foot. The woman claims she was walking in the town square when a man grabbed her leg, fell to the ground and began sniffing her shoe. The publicity surrounding this latest attack reportedly encouraged another victim to come forward. The second woman, who was attacked last Autumn, said her experience was exactly the same. "The only thing I could do was get my foot out of my shoe and then I ran away. I looked back and he was just lying in the mud with my shoe," she concluded.

Robbers Caught While Taking Coffee Break

KUALA LUMPUR, Malaysia - A gang of four men responsible for 20 cases of motorcycle theft, rape, and armed robbery were caught taking a coffee break this week immediately after robbing a mobile phone shop. The foursome held two employees at gunpoint and took an unsubstantiated number of phones and cash before escaping. But they didn't get too far. The owner was about to fill out a police report when he noticed the thieves' car at a nearby drink stall. The owner contacted the police, and they arrested the four without any problems. Fleeing the scene did not make it high on the priority list for this foursome.

Justice Has A Long Memory

ALBUQUERQUE, New Mexico - A convicted killer who escaped from a New Mexico prison more than 20 years ago has finally been caught. Clarence McCoy pleaded guilty in 1978 to strangling his wife. He was serving a 10-year sentence when he escaped from a state prison south of Albuquerque. He was 27 at the time. Retribution finally caught up with the killer when he compounded his crime by driving alone in a car pool lane in Washington state. During the traffic stop, McCoy's name was put through a computer background check which produced his criminal background. He is fighting extradition to New Mexico.

Convict Gives Police Slip with Fake ID

LOS ANGELES, California - Police were searching for a Los Angeles County jail inmate who escaped with the help of a forged ID card with the picture of actor Eddie Murphy. A swarm of police conducted a yard-by-yard search when the escape was discovered but the suspect was long gone. Informants have told investigators that Kevin J. Pullum, 31, - who was jailed on attempted murder charges - forged an ID card that looked like the cards used by civilian employees of the jail. The card featured a photo that was clipped from a magazine ad for *Dr. Dolittle 2*. Much of the escape was recorded on the jail's video system that showed Pullum nonchalantly strolling out of custody.

"Not Guilty" Tattoo Pegs Man Guilty

LONG BEACH, Mississippi - Police in Long Beach, Miss., say a would-be robber was apprehended by a police detective because of a distinctive tattoo. The man rushed into a convenience store demanding $200 he had allegedly left on the counter earlier. When the cashier told him all the money was already locked in the safe, he pulled a gun but ran when more customers entered the store. The clerk gave police a description, noting his large tattoo bearing the words: "NOT GUILTY." The next morning the man went to the same store, still demanding his money. A detective was there doing some shopping and recognized the tattoo from an "all points bulletin." The man was arrested on a charge of attempted armed robbery. "His tattoo stuck out like a sore thumb," the officer told the *Sun Herald* newspaper. "He might as well have had "STUPID" printed on his forehead."

Devil Worshipper Charged with Grave Robbing

BRAINTREE, Massachusetts - Police in a town just south of Boston received a tip that George Picard, 34, had allegedly stolen items from his upstairs neighbor. When they searched Picard's apartment, they found several alarming objects including a skull, bones, a brain and a fetus in jars, as well as occult paraphernalia. Picard has been charged with grave robbing and drug possession. Police Lt. Russell Jenkins told a local newspaper that the man is suspected to be involved in devil worship, and neighbors said he had "mental problems." The skull allegedly was stolen from a nearby cemetery, while the fetus and brain apparently were stolen from the New England Medical Center in Boston, where Picard had worked as an electrician.

A Lawsuit of 'Sizable' Proportions

MEXICO CITY - A burglar in Mexico City was in for a big surprise when he broke into the home of 350-pound Maria Teresina-Lorca. Miguel Pintado, 42, has filed a lawsuit against Teresina-Lorca for using "excessive force" when she apparently assaulted him and proceeded to sit upon him for a half-hour while waiting for the police to arrive. Pintado said he suffered a fractured rib as well as severe emotional trauma from "being smothered under the flabby buttocks of that big woman for so long." In order to compensate for the incident, he is asking for the equivalent of $300,000 in damages.

Escapee Back Behind Bars

LOS ANGELES, California - We recently ran a story about a clever convict who escaped from Los Angeles County jail using a forged ID card bearing the picture of actor Eddie Murphy. A chance encounter with police on Los Angeles's skid row landed the elusive fugitive back in jail 16 days after his escape. LA police patrolling the downtown area spotted the escapee, Kevin Pullum, seated on a milk crate peddling alcoholic cold drinks to transients just a couple of miles from the "Twin Towers" jail he escaped from. He was carrying yet another false identification.
[Hey, go with what works.]

Man Fakes His Death and Is Sentenced for Fraud

BRIDGEPORT, Connecticut - A financial advisor in Connecticut faked his own death to claim $7 million from an insurance policy. To simulate his body, Madison Rutherford, 39, robbed a grave of human bones and teeth. He put the bones, teeth, and his wristwatch in a burnt out car and has been declared dead since a 1998 accident on a freeway in Mexico. When his widow immediately tried to collect the $7 million, the insurance company decided to investigate Rutherford's death. An anthropologist found that the bones actually belong to an American Indian at least 20 years older than him. Rutherford has plead guilty for fraud and is in jail. His wife will be sentenced next for her involvement.

Judge Rules Over Finger Fetish With an Iron Fist

BURNSVILLE, Minnesota - Most people get out of the thumb sucking stage as a toddler. But Richard Lee Sanders's alleged finger-sucking fetish has brought him a fist full of trouble. The 38-year-old has been charged with three counts of disorderly conduct in Dakota County District Court for sucking the fingers of women in Burnsville and Apple Valley. He had been charged with the same offense in June. Sanders supposedly approached women at a business, remarked that their nails were pretty and asked if they were real. Then he stuck them in his mouth before they could react. Burnsville prosecutor Michael Mayer stated that this was "his weirdest case in his 16 years on the job."

Robber Stops to Order a Burger to Go

MANCHESTER, Connecticut - Apparently criminals have to eat, too. A robber held up a popular fast food chain at gunpoint, then ordered the cook to prepare him a Whopper with extra cheese. The gunman reportedly walked into the fast food shop in Manchester, Connecticut, and went straight to the restroom. Moments later he walked back up front wearing a bandana over his face and brandishing a hand gun. He proceeded to herd the crew into a walk-in freezer and then took the manager to open the safe. With the money in hand, he walked the manager back to the freezer, then told the cook to come out and ordered him to make him a Whopper with cheese. Police are still trying to find the thief before he runs out of money or the next snack attack occurs.

5

Wild Kingdom: Animals in the Bizarre

With roughly 800,000 species the Animal Kingdom can be weird enough. But it's when you mix it with the weirdest animal of all, man, that animals earn their own chapter in Bizarre News. Welcome to the wild kingdom where bizarre animal acts run rampant. This crazy chapter includes everything from pigs having sex on the Internet to roosters working out on treadmills. Don't miss some bizarre twists of fate, too. In one story, a python dies because a man bites IT. And you'll learn the meaning of "poetic justice" when you read about the sacrificial lamb who butts his owner off a rooftop to avoid slaughter. Now that's what I call taking the initiative.

Dog Enlightened During a Walk in the Park

CHICAGO, Illinois - Dogs generally "light up" when their owner offers to take them for a walk in the park. However, Portia, a 5-year-old black Labrador retriever, was in for quite a "shock" during her walk with owner Kerry Sorvino. As the 70-pound canine stepped onto a metal plate covering an electrical vault on the sidewalk, it began to convulse uncontrollably as a voltage of electricity surged through its body. Sorvino, not knowing what was wrong, bent over to calm the squealing pooch which bit her on the hand. A passerby summoned a veterinarian from an animal hospital and he tried to give Portia mouth-to-mouth resuscitation. However, he kept getting a shock from her lips and was unable to save her. City officials said a frayed wire apparently contacted the cover plate set into the sidewalk on Wrightwood near Lincoln and Sheffield.

Sacrificial Lamb Tells Owner To Take a Dive

ALEXANDRIA, Egypt - A sacrificial lamb told its owner in its own words to eat "sheep" and die. Waheeb Hamoudah plummeted to his death when the sheep that he had been fattening up for the past six weeks on his rooftop butted him off. The 56-year-old worked in the police tax evasion department and planned to kill the lamb for Eid al-Adha, the Muslim feast of sacrifice, in early March. Neighbors found Hamoudah lying bleeding on the ground below, with several broken bones. He died soon after reaching hospital.

Elephant Refuses to Let Go of Main Squeeze

GUWAHATI, India - Elephants are said not to forget and evidently are not much for letting things go, either. According to police in northeast India, a wild elephant pulled a man down from a tree, trampled him to death and has refused to part with the corpse for two weeks. The man climbed the tree to escape a herd of wild elephants rampaging through his village about 80 miles from Guwahati, the largest city in Assam. One elephant grabbed the man, pulled him to the ground and broke his legs. It then trampled him and took the body along with him. It has not been determined as to how authorities plan to get the corpse away from the protective pachyderm.

Man Becomes Pain in Neck for Snake

PRETORIA, South Africa - Here's a switch. A deadly rock python died after a 57-year-old man bit him in the neck. Council worker Lucas Sibanda was walking to his Pretoria home when the snake slithered from some shrubs and began wrapping itself around him. Deciding retaliation was his only chance of survival, he sunk his teeth into the python's neck, then kicked and punched it until the snake finally untangled itself. After the snake let go, Sibanda said he hit it with a stick before it could attack him again. He has reportedly skinned the python and says he will leave it outside his house as proof for people who might not believe his story.

Sex-Starved Pooch Pins Postman For Smooch

LOCH NESS, Scotland - It seems that the mythical Loch Ness Monster is not the only thing to be leery of in Scotland. Postman Phil Rose was pinned to the ground by a 196-pound, sex-starved Newfoundland dog named Bruno. Rose, who is only 154 pounds himself, was attacked by the amorous pooch while making a delivery to the Lock Inn pub. Bruno's owner, James MacLennan, witnessed the "attack" from an upstairs window, but said he was laughing too much to rescue him. "Before Phil could get up, Bruno was on top of him, his legs wrapped around him, furiously licking his face - and a good bit more besides," laughed MacLennan. About 10 minutes later he managed to get the pooch off him and sped off in his van. "I must really try and get Bruno a girlfriend," MacLennan concluded.

Ape Escapes for Human Food

PITTSBURGH, Pennsylvania - The grass might not have been green-
er on the other the side of the fence, but perhaps the food was better!
A 150-pound gorilla escaped from her pen and dined on food from
some of the half-finished plates at the zoo's concession area for about
45 minutes recently before she was lured into the women's restroom
and tranquilized. No one was injured.
[When asked, zookeepers were said to have overheard the ape saying... "I'm mad as hell and I'm not going to take it anymore!"]

The World's Heaviest Raccoon Gets Even Heavier

PALMERTON, Pennsylvania - In another Bizarre Animal Story we
are fascinated by Bandit, the Guinness Book of World Records holder
of the feat...World's Heaviest Raccoon. But now there is cause for
alarm as Bandit just keeps getting bigger! Weighing in at 64.9 pounds,
owner Deborah Klitsch has tried putting the blubbery Bandit on a diet,
but the beachball-sized creature doesn't like the dry cat food she gives
him, so he frequently "gets in the cabinets and goes after (potato)
chips," she said. "Now the vet thinks he may have an inactive thyroid."

Birds to be Charged with Flying Under the Influence

REDDING, California - Flocks of drunken birds have ruffled many
motorists' feathers along Interstate 5 in California. The birds had
apparently been eating the parneyi cotoneaster berry, a fermenting
fruit that gives birds an alcohol buzz. While "flying under the influence," our feathered friends frequently collide with car windshields
and crash into the pavement, leaving a trail of bird carcasses all over
the highway. California Highway Patrol spokesman Monty Hite
chided, "They're not buying into the 'designated flier' program, either,
and the T-shirts don't fit them."

The Future Crocodile Hunter?

AUSTRALIA - Steve Irwin listen up, there could be a new "Crocodile Hunter" in the ranks. Sam West, 12, reportedly escaped the jaws of a fourteen-foot crocodile by biting its nose and gouging its eye with his fingers. West claims he learned this technique by watching the feature film *Deep Blue Sea*, where a swimmer escaped from a shark by stabbing it in the eye with a cross. The attack happened while Sam was snorkeling in North West Australia. Crocodile expert Graham Webb stated that the boy was lucky to be alive, because the croc could have gone into what is known as a "death roll" and drowned the boy before he had a chance to fight it off.

You've Reached Spot's Stomach. He's Not Available...

MOMBASSA, Kenya - Kamal Shah lost his mobile phone. Most people would probably search their homes, cars or workplaces. In fact, Shah thought he had left it on his bedside table and presumed his son had taken it. However, the phone turned up in the unlikeliest spot. When he called the mobile number from his regular line, his dog's stomach started ringing. The event was so unexpected Shah commented, "It sent me into shock." The German Shepherd named Snoopy had swallowed it. During an operation, the phone was removed.

I Smell a Rat!

SOUTH AFRICA - Here is one to make your skin crawl. A South African couple has been using their home to breed hundreds of rats and are now being ordered to destroy them. One officer reported, "There were holes in the floor and rats everywhere. We thought there was a person under the duvet, but it turned out to be more rats. They'd even eaten the bed." Environmental health officers have ordered the couple to kill the rats or find them a proper home.

Baaaaad Lamb Shoots Sleeping Shepard

SIDI BARRANI, Egypt - Next time you lay down to take a nap among your flock of sheep, make sure none of them has a grudge against you. Egyptian shepherd Mokhtar Adam Fadl should have followed this advice for he was shot dead - by one of his own sheep - while he slept. According to the police, the animal killed Fadl by kicking his gun and accidentally firing it. The shot hit the slumbering sheep herder in the chest. The gun was reportedly confiscated. No arrests were made.

New Hobby: Collecting Deformed Animals

WISCONSIN - Farmer Paul Springer has been trading unusual and deformed animals since the 1970s when he purchased a six-legged calf. He displayed Ole' Bessie at state fairs and had her stuffed after she died. The farmer learns of deformed animals like two-headed calves and a donkey with one head and two bodies from livestock dealers and other farmers. He then sells the animals to circuses and freak shows. If he is particularly fond of them, he stuffs the animals when they die and displays them at his farm. Springer does not accept just any deformity, though. He has turned down a cow without a tail before, saying it wasn't unusual enough. The farmer's last name is so fitting...

Man Admits to Banging His Dog

CAROLINE COUNTY - When police went to 33-year-old David Lee's house to search for drugs, they were in for a bizarre surprise. In addition to finding more than 81 ounces of marijuana and 9.55 grams of cocaine, Commonwealth Attorney Harvey Latney reports they also discovered a home video of Lee having sex with his beagle. Lee later confirmed the tape and plead guilty to the drug charges and carnal knowledge of an animal. The latter has a maximum sentence of five years in jail, and Lee will be sentenced in June. Even man's best friend has to draw the line somewhere.

Thirsty Chimp Gets Drunk at 'Monkey Bar?'

HUNGARY - If one were to open a new pub in the animal kingdom, and name it "The Monkey Bar," Johnny the chimp would certainly be a regular patron. The thirsty little chimp, along with his partner, Zsiga, both escaped from their cage after the lock had been removed by an unknown person. The feisty duo allegedly attacked a 60-year-old woman who tried to hinder their escape and later wrestled with a man who tried to grab them in Budapest. Fire officers were able to recapture Johnny by feeding him beers until he passed out. Zsiga was knocked out cold after running head on into a glass door. According to the chimps' trainer, Lajos Korosi, "They both have very sore heads, and we are leaving them to take their bad tempers out on each other for a few days."

Live Sex on the Internet!

AUSTRIA - A new reality show began this week on the Internet. The show promises to broadcast contestants having sex and going hog wild. "Temptation Island II," you ask? Not in this case - the contestants are pigs. The sites stars, Fred, Oscar, Joseph, Junior, Lulu and Xanophela, have been so popular that people have been logging on like crazy to see the pigs get some. Viewers choose their favorites, and the winning pig is promised a long and blissful existence by the Austrian Young Farmer's Association. A sequel is already in the works called "Girls Camp," featuring cows. The association said in an official statement, "Austria's farmers have nothing to hide. We hope that this project can give everyone the possibility to get to know our agriculture." Because we couldn't have just read a brochure.

Alcoholic Elephants Force Villagers into Trees

NEW DELHI, India - In the eastern Indian state of Orissa, over 60 elephants are experiencing withdrawal. According to an official source, the elephants are rampaging thought the area, following the waft of homemade liquor. They run around crazily sniffing for the drink, simultaneously forcing two dozen tribes people to seek retreat and slumber in treetops. In the meantime, the elephants have damaged mud houses in their path. The smell of handia, a local brew made out of rice, has drawn the elephants from around the area. According to Ashok Meena, Keonjhar District Magistrate, "Close to two dozen people are staying in the treetops with family members because they're afraid of the elephants. They often take bedding and food during the night."

Brew-Loving Bat Trapped in Beer Bottle

BROCKLEHURST, New South Wales - Too much alcohol will make anyone batty, but what do bats get when they are drunk? One poor little creature became intoxicated after becoming trapped in a beer bottle in Australia. He must have had one heck of a hangover because he spent a week recovering from the ordeal in the care of a local vet. No one knows why the bat chose to go into the bottle in the first place. According to Dennis Whitton, who helped take care of the bat, "It's not like beer is a natural part of a bat's diet. I have to say a beer bottle is the strangest."

Lean, Mean Cock-Fighting Machines

BANGKOK, Thailand - In the old days, roosters prepared for their big cock fights by simply racing against one another. Not anymore. Farmer Thaweechai Thongruay has invented a treadmill specially designed for the little warriors. Each treadmill is 15 inches wide, 25 inches long and 35 inches high. The roosters' exercise regimen begins with five to 10 minutes on the treadmill until they can build their endurance to a desired 30-minute workout. Thongruay defended his product, saying "Roosters that have been trained on the treadmills are fully fit. When they get in the ring, their legs are strong and they never stop the footwork." Cockfighting is illegal in many countries including the United States.

Oscar the Grouchy Swan

OSLO, Norway - The infamously ill-tempered swan named Oscar was having a rotten day when Kerstin Arbsved approached his lake with her family. The grouchy swan attacked the elderly lady, biting and dragging her into the water. Arbsved gave Reuters the details, "Oscar came flying from across the other side of the lake and bit me in the buttocks before dragging me about five meters into the water and under." He halted the attack when her daughter threw rocks at him. Oscar was put down when police and medical staff came to the scene, and Arbsved recovered nicely in a hospital overnight.

Here Be Dragons

LOS ANGELES ZOO, California - *San Francisco Chronicle* executive editor Phil Bronstein was attacked by a Komodo dragon last week during a visit to the LA Zoo. Bronstein's wife, actress Sharon Stone, had arranged a private tour of the zoo as a Father's Day surprise. The highlight of the day was going to be an up-close visit with one of the giant lizards with which Bronstein has had a long-time fascination. Bronstein was asked to take off his white shoes before entering the cage to keep the 5-foot-long reptile from mistaking them for the white rats it is fed. The strategy did not work as the dragon lunged for one of his feet and nearly managed to take off Bronstein's big toe. Doctors were able to rebuild most of the toe. The dragon was not injured.

Snake Bite Is Worth A Thousand Words

SOUTH CAROLINA - A man tried to take a picture of his "pet" snake, a deadly Asiatic spitting cobra, but was bitten on the thumb in the process. Teddy Terrants, 21, was paralyzed and on a ventilator before being flown to Kendall Regional Medical Center Thursday and administered the anti-venom. He did not regain consciousness until after receiving 10 vials of the anti-venom. He said at first the bite felt like a bee sting. "I didn't feel nothing. I sat down. I was under the air condition(er). I just started sweating," he said. The man refuses to blame his pet snake. "Not the snake's fault. My fault. I shouldn't have been messing around his pen," he said. Terrants' wife is nine months pregnant and wants to get rid of the snake. He refuses.

Unnecessary Snake Bites Part II

COLOMBIA - A man was working in a Colombian field when he realized he had to urinate. He was relieving himself behind a nearby bush when a Mapana Tiger snake leapt up and bit his penis. Alarmed by his frantic screams, his wife rushed him to the hospital. The victim received anti-poison drugs and is currently recovering. A doctor said, "He's very lucky to have survived the accident as that kind of snake is very dangerous."

Fiery Fax Spells Disaster for a Family in Norway

SENJAHOPEN, Norway - Some cats are said to be full of piss and vinegar, but I bet a family in Norway never believed that could be such an explosive combination. Home and pet owner Asle Reieertsen arrived home to find a smoke-filled kitchen after his cat, Fax, urinated on an electric socket and caused a short circuit. Reieertsen was able to disconnect the fuse and avert serious damages to his home. The cat reportedly was unharmed in the incident.

Prayerful Pooch Never Misses Church

LISBON, Portugal - Preta the pooch never misses a Sunday service at her local Catholic church. Every Sunday morning at 5:00, the dog leaves her owner's house in the small town of Sobrado and trots to the neighboring village of Ermesinde for church, about eight miles away. Preta saunters right up to the church's chancel and lies down by the side of the altar. When the congregants rise for the Kyrie or the Gospel lesson, so does she. When they sit down, she'll stretch out on the stone floor again. The church is routinely packed to capacity because everyone wants to see the famous parishioner.

Going Hog Wild

BRANDENBURG, Germany - A pair of pigs in Germany went absolutely hog wild in an area supermarket. German police answered a call about a break-in and found the scintillating swine pigging out on biscuits. The wild boars reportedly smashed through the glass doors while the Brandenburg shop was shut. One of the pigs appeared to have injured itself on the broken glass door.

Florida Woman Takes No Bull from Canine

TALLAHASSEE, Florida - An elderly woman decided to bite the "bull"et in an effort to save her little Scots terrier. Margaret Hargrove, 73, was out for an evening stroll with her dog, Alex, when they were attacked by a pit bull. As the ferocious canine clamped its jaws around the young pup's head, Hargrove got down on her hands and knees and bit the pit bull in the back of the neck. The pit bull reportedly let go of the smaller dog and backed off, then bared its teeth at Hargrove, who attacked the dog again. A neighbor soon arrived with a baseball bat to scare off the pit bull. Hargrove needed four stitches in her arm. Her dog also needed stitches.

Birds of a Feather...

VALPARAISO, Indiana - A maid was in the middle of completing her regular cleaning routine when she found blood and chicken feathers all over a room in a Valparaiso motel. She immediately alerted hotel officials, who determined the room had been rented the night before by Michael Bessigano, 30. Police were called to the scene and reported that Bessigano had a history of sexually abusing animals ranging from geese to dogs. The suspect admitted to stealing the chicken from a farm south of town and said he had sex with it. Bessigano now faces up to seven-and-a-half years in prison. The chicken did not survive the experience.

Scientists Give Sheep Baaaaad Shakes

NEW YORK - I hope this won't give sex toy makers any more brilliant ideas. Scientists at the State University of New York at Stony Brook have reportedly been vibrating sheep in search for a cure for osteoporosis. Research shows bursts of high-frequency vibration can help prevent brittle bone disease. To test their theory, scientists mechanically stimulated the hind limbs of adult sheep every day for a year by standing them on a vibrating platform for 20 minutes. At the end of the study, the density of spongy bone in the animals' thighs was 34% higher than in sheep not receiving the treatment.

Man Uses Cow's Butt to Sneak Tobacco Into Prison

INDIANA - An Indiana man's plan to smuggle tobacco into prison by hiding it inside cows' rectums went up in smoke. Former warden John Hester, 51, had the responsibility of bringing the cows to the Pendleton prison and killing them for regular consumption within the compound. Hester was trying to trade the tobacco for money orders obtained for him by an inmate's mother. Now out on bail, Hester faces seven charges of bribery and is awaiting trial. In an attempt to explain the complicated smuggling process, Indiana State Police Detective Gregory Belt stated, "It was stuffed into the cow, and then the cow was brought onto the floor and it was removed."

[Thanks for that moooooving testimony, Detective.]

Sampson the Swan Receives Bionic Bill

AMROTH, Wales - Sampson the swan's bill was severely damaged when someone attacked the bird with a bottle. Maria Evans, who runs a bird rescue center, adopted the swan and struck on an ingenious plan to save it. She asked Dentist Ed Hannaford to create a plastic bill of sorts for the swan so he would not have to eat from a tube for the remainder of his days. Hannaford spent over 100 hours building the first-ever bionic beak, fitted perfectly for Sampson. The creation was a success as eight-year-old Sampson was eating and kissing his mate just an hour after the fitting. Evans said, "It is a miracle. Sampson is now fighting-fit."

UFB (Unidentified Flying Bovine)

ANKARA, Turkey - Ethem Sahin was inside a coffee house having an espresso when witnesses say a cow fell through the roof knocking him unconscious. "My friends told me later what happened. I couldn't believe it," Sahin told reporters. Sahin's wife was just as astounded. "They told me that a cow fell on top of my husband. I thought they were kidding me. May God protect us from a worse accident," she said. Apparently, the cow wandered from the hillside where it was grazing onto the roof of the coffee house, which was built into the side of the hill. Sahin was treated for minor injuries including a broken leg. The cow was mostly unharmed.

6

Don't Break My Heart

What could be better than the butterflies in your stomach when you see your soul mate? Ah love, isn't it grand? Well, not for the people in this chapter. Don't take any relationship advice from the woman who successfully killed her husband on the seventh try. Or from the wife who chopped off her husband's right hand (he stayed with her, by the way). Men, listen up - when your significant other wants a little action, just give it to her. Take it from the husband whose wife burned him with an iron because he fell asleep without giving her some nookie! Don't miss the story of the man who rented out his girlfriend to a millionaire to help pay for a medical procedure or the one about a wife selling her husband to his mistress over the Internet. Hell hath no fury like a woman scorned...

Father of 42 Ready to Tie the Knot Again

BEIRUT - After exhausting three wives and fathering 42 children, a love-crazed Lebanese farmer will take another wife in a few weeks to keep up with his insatiable sexual appetite. The 47-year-old Lebanese farmer got married for the first time in his 20s. A few years and a dozen children later, his wife felt he was getting bored with her so she set him up with a second woman. The second wife then bore Abdel-Al at least a dozen more babies, and then she told him to marry a third woman. According to Abdel-Al, "Allah ordered us to love each other and I love women. I can't live without love, or at least without women." Islam allows men to take up to four wives.

Another Marriage Shot to Hell

GILLINGHAM, UK - Some marriages just go to hell in a hand basket. Paul Sainsbury and Lynda Eastwood are petitioning authorities for permission to have a satanic wedding to ensure theirs does, literally. The pair have been told by their local council that it has "in principle, no objection" to the wedding - even though it involves the drinking of "blood" red wine while those present lift their arms to the sky saying, "Bless you, Father Satan, I will always love you". The damned couple met last year at an Iron Maiden concert and say they are looking forward to their midnight union in August.

Men Put Off When Girls Wanna Have Fun - With One Another

LAWRENCE, Missouri - Police officers were called to intervene when two men started fighting after their girlfriends showed more interest in each other than in them. The two couples had been for a night out and returned home whereupon the two women reportedly went into the bedroom and "became friendly." After their request to join in was declined, the two men started fighting and fell through a glass door.

Jam Inheritance Proves To Be Grave Matter

ROMANIA - A 37-year-old Romanian sought revenge against his recently deceased mother-in-law after learning she bequeathed him a single pot of jam in her will. Claudiu Vlad, from Buzau, got back at his mother-in-law by selling her grave to unsuspecting neighbor Costel Petrache without telling him that Roxana Petrescu's body was still in it. However, Petrache discovered the body two weeks later after his own father died and is now suing Vlad for fraud.

Seventh Time is the Charm for Vengeful Wife

TAIPAI, Taiwan - The seventh time was the charm for a woman in Taiwan who finally succeeded in killing her husband by burning him alive. Earlier failed attempts include a stabbing, a poisoning and a bogus car crash. Liao Je-hung told a Taiwan court she set out to kill her husband, Lin Jung-lo, because of his womanizing and miserliness. She then told them with this final attempt she hired a hit man that got her husband drunk, took him to the river and set him ablaze. Both she and the killer she hired have been jailed for life for the murder. The other failed killers were jailed for up to 18 years.

Jolie Makes Bloody Mess on Set of *Tomb Raider*

HOLLYWOOD, California - Just when the Angelina Jolie incest rumors had quieted, the rebellious daughter of John Voight strikes again. The actress reportedly showed up at a recent photo shoot with several wounds on her arms. She allegedly explained that the marks were cuts she made before having sex. She also reportedly wore a glass pendant containing blood from her actor-husband Billy Bob Thornton. According to the *New York Post*, Jolie refused to wear the clothes costumers had chosen for her on the *Tomb Raider* set. When she finally conceded, she still refused to remove the pendant claiming, "This is my husband's blood!"

Murder and Conspiracy In Troy, Michigan

TROY, Michigan - Billie Jean Rogers, 61, is charged with first-degree murder in suburban Detroit, Michigan, for smothering her husband. The victim, Donald Rogers, 74, had a high alcohol content at the time of his death, as well as a pre-existing heart problem. Thus, the cause of his death was originally undetermined. However, an accomplice to the murder eventually leaked the details of the crime. Billie Jean Rogers and her nephew, now Vonlee Titlow, 33 of Chicago, allegedly plotted to murder the husband to obtain money for a sex change operation for him. After the death, Billie Jean Rogers gave Titlow $70,000 for the operation and a luxury sedan. Titlow, who has now also been charged with first-degree murder, slipped the details to a man she was dating. And you thought Jerry Springer was fake.

Mistress Buys Lover from His Wife for Bargain

HANOI, Vietnam - This could be the hot new item on eBay: cheating spouses. After a failed attempt to persuade her husband to give up his younger mistress, a Vietnamese woman reportedly decided to sell him to his lover for only $516. The younger woman paid the fuming wife the lump sum and immediately set up home with the husband. It is reported that the new couple is getting along well and the 41-year-old wife is now living alone.

Husband Stays with Wife After Fatal Attraction

NEW DELHI, India - A 37-year-old bus driver in New Delhi was asleep when his wife chopped off his right hand. The couple had fought earlier that night. Husband Rajkumar said, "We had an argument about our different castes, and she threw a stone at my head." He then slapped her and left to go drinking at a nearby bar. His wife pounced after he passed out at home later. His hand was reattached in a 12-hour emergency operation. It was not the first time she attacked, though. His wife Rajvanti bit off half his left ear two years ago, but he still withdrew his police statement. Can anyone say "Fatal Attraction?" Rajvanti is now dutifully at her husband's bedside during the recuperation period.

A Prostitute By Any Other Name...

GERMANY - Prostitutes and pimps come in various forms. When German folk pop singer Christian Anders, 56, found out he needed a liver transplant, he was unsure how to fund the expense. Thank goodness he had a young girlfriend. Anders is renting out his girlfriend Jenna Kartes, 20, for a year to millionaire Michael Leicher. The contracted settlement is for $231,000 with a renewal option after a year. Though she was shocked, Kartes remains accepting and optimistic about the trade. She stated, "I will sleep with Michael because I love Christian. Perhaps he can afford a new liver. Why should I feel like a prostitute about it?" Let's call a spade a spade, folks.

I Take This Woman and This Woman to Be My Wife

PROVO, Utah - In order to receive official statehood, Utah outlawed polygamy over 100 years ago. However, the state government frequently turns a blind eye on the practice. Enter polygamy poster boy Tom Green. He has simultaneously had five wives and is being charged with four counts of bigamy and criminal non-support. One of his wives was only 13 years old at the time of the union, so Green may consequently face child rape charges, too. According to local newspapers and court hearings, Green made a habit of marrying one wife, divorcing her, then marrying the next one, all the while still living with his previous wives. He is expecting his 30th child from the group in June. The polygamist believes it is a spiritual practice and is willing to do jail time for the cause.

Zip Your Lips!

HANOI, Vietnam - Giving new meaning to the time-honored command "zip your lips," a couple was recently sent to jail in Vietnam for mistreating a ten-year-old boy. When the boy stole the equivalent of 1.3 cents last month, his stepmother, Phan Thi Hien, 31, made him sew his lips together with a needle and thread. She has been sentenced to 30 months in jail, but her husband received a sentence of 12 months.

I Object - The Groom Is Actually a Woman!

MAFIKENG, South Africa - A love-struck couple was in the middle of exchanging wedding vows when officials intervened, claiming the groom's birth certificate listed him as female. As the wedding was stopped, a stunned silence engulfed the room. According to *The Citizen* newspaper, the couple must indefinitely postpone the ceremony. Rankoa Molefe, the groom, unknowingly had the birth certificate with the error for 12 years and said the incident "was terribly upsetting and embarrassing." Molefe must have a doctor declare him a male before the birth certificate can be changed. The home affairs minister told the groom the document will be changed, to which he replied, "It's a relief to be a man again."

Groom and Best Man Turn into Human Souffles

WILTSHIRE, England - Most bachelor parties consist of drinking, strippers, and last-minute shenanigans. An English groom-to-be and his best man were recent victims of such a stag party prank as they were abandoned on the Warminster bypass in Wiltshire. The two 20-something men were handcuffed together, drenched in eggs, flour, and tomato sauce, and left in the stifling heat. Officers took them to the police station where they could clean up and described the two as having "all the ingredients for a good souffle." They gave the victims directions to the nearest train station and sent them on their way. One police representative said, "Officers did not know what to make of it."

Wife's Fiery Hot Temper Causes $65,000 in Damages

PANAMA CITY, Florida - A heated dispute got a lot hotter when a woman in Panama City decided to set one of her husband's shirts on fire. Sharon Kirkman's temper was not the only thing flaring when the blaze spread and burned down the whole house. She was charged with arson and her little tirade is estimated to cost approximately $65,000 in damages. According to Don Cieota, an investigator with the state fire marshal's office, their insurance company is not going to cover the fire because it was started by one of the owners.

Divorce Lawyers Take Note

UNITED ARAB EMIRATES - A whole new arena of marital law has been ushered into existence. In the Gulf emirate of Dubai men can now use mobile phone text messages to divorce their wives. Under strict interpretation of Islamic law, a man can divorce his wife simply by saying "I divorce thee" three times. Islamic religious scholars have now decreed that a text message is a valid way of ending a marriage. The ruling follows a case in which a woman received a text message from her husband saying: "You are divorced because you are late."

Priest Gives Newlywed Couple His Own "Blessing"

INDEPENDENTA, Romania - It almost turned into a triple burial when an Orthodox priest and his mistress were thrown naked out of a house by her husband - right in the middle of a funeral procession. The 35-year-old priest had married the young woman to her husband three weeks earlier. The lovers were caught by the husband at his home in County Galati. Church authorities are now investigating the incident.

Yeah, But All The Witnesses Are Dead

13,000 FEET BELOW SEA-LEVEL - A New York couple plans to be married aboard a mini submarine perched on the sunken remains of the Titanic, some 2.5 miles beneath the Atlantic Ocean. Groom David Leibowitz won a competition offering a dive to the Titanic organized by British diving company SubSea Explorer. It seemed perfectly natural to him to ask his fiancee to go down with him and exchange their vows on the deck of the doomed liner. The expedition is said to cost $560,000. The bodies of 1,500 people are still on board the ship. [Talk about an unlucky way to start a marriage. Personally, I think a graveyard would be easier.]

Newlywed Has Iron-Clad Plan To Heat Up Love Life

ANDRIASU, Romania - Some issues should have been "ironed out" before the wedding takes place. Mircea Stoleru learned this the hard way after his 18-year-old wife burned him with a hot iron because he fell asleep without making love to her. The young woman apparently was not too pleased and decided to heat things up a bit by scorching her husband on the right shoulder with the heated appliance. Stoleru told reporters, "This should serve me right. I knew what I got when I married such a young and beautiful wife, and I never get home sober."

Ads Ask Wives to Have Husbands Stop Visiting Prostitutes

CZECHOSLOVAKIA - The mayors of several Czech towns have planned an aggressive ad campaign targeting women shoppers in Austria. A highway traveling north through the Czech Republic is flanked by prostitutes, and the mayors estimate that over 95% of the customers are Austrian men. This new billboard ad campaign will instruct the Austrian wives who shop in the Republic to stop their husbands from illegally cavorting with the prostitutes. Mayor of Dolni Dvoriste, Emil Ruzicka, said "Many Austrian women come shopping here, so they'll see these posters." Deputy mayor of Kaplice Jan Kozojed said, "If we can stop the demand from the Austrian side, then the supply of prostitutes will also stop."

Size Doesn't Really Matter in Nigerian Court

NIGERIA - According to a court in Nigeria, the size of a man's penis is not grounds for a divorce. Amina Haruna tried to leave her husband, Malam Hassan Mujahid, due to the fact that his penis was too big for them to have sex without injuring her. A higher sharia court in the city of Gusau, Zamfara State, ordered the 22-year-old to return to her husband on the grounds that Mujahid's penis was normal-sized.

French Kissing Lands German Couple in Lake

LUDWIGSHAFEN, Germany - An amorous German couple became a little too preoccupied in their make-out session to realize their car was rolling into the lake they were parked in front of. According to police in the town of Ludwigshafen, the couple was engaged in "interpersonal activities" when one of them accidentally knocked the handbrake, unlocking it. With nothing hurt but their pride, the couple watched as firefighters towed their car out of the lake.

Woman Says Reach Out and Touch This

TAIWAN - A Taiwanese woman learned the hard way how not to reach out to touch someone. Doctors at the Taipei Medical University hospital had to surgically remove a Nokia cell phone from the 20-year-old's rectum after it became stuck there during a bizarre sex game with her boyfriend. Hospital staffers speculated that the phone was used as a stimulatory device because of its vibrating feature.

7

Greetings Fellow Bizarros

I have always enjoyed the editorial portion of Bizarre News because it allows me to become involved with some of the stories rather than just reporting on them. In this, the interaction with readers has been invaluable. As my network of contacts has grown I have found myself drawn into some really bizarre adventures. Traveling around the country following the clues of Bizarre readers, and even peeking at the subculture in my own city has provided some of the best columns I have written for this publication. If you had told me fifteen years ago that I would be researching monster stories, going under cover at survival camps or interviewing porno actresses for a living, I would have called you a liar. But as the saying goes, "There is no teacher like experience!"

Greetings Fellow Bizarros:

Going "undercover" in the porn industry is no picnic. I thought that it would be amusing, but it is a world unlike anything I have EVER seen before. The first thing I did is unsubscribe my wife from this publication. I figure I could feign mailing problems until the assignment is over.

I arrived in a Chicago warehouse that had been turned into a "studio". I thought my job was to hold a boom for the shooting, but I became a "gopher" with two other guys. One was named "Robert" and the other was named "Neil". I could not resist going into my Andrew Dice Clay mode and said, "Hey, Neil and Bob, are those your names or is that what you guys do?" I thought it was funny. They did not appreciate my sense of humor.

The name of the movie being shot is a take off on *Gladiator* called, *Glad He Ate Her*. Amusing and creative, but I doubt that this will be in a theater near you anytime soon. They are shooting this in video and in three days, the movie will be done.

There are people everywhere. The actresses are beautiful and do not seem to know or even care how exploited they are. But it is the men who are the most ridiculous figures in these movies. They have a room that is called "the warm up room" where men go to prepare themselves for the upcoming shots. This preparation often requires various forms of stimulation called "Fluffs" to reach the necessary level of excitement (I never went into the room, this is what Neil told me.)

The director is a hoot. He thinks he is making *Gone With The Wind*. He actually was speaking with one of the ladies about her motivation for the scene. In the scene, she was thrown into a dungeon to service one of the victors from a battle. Not being a filmmaker, I think her motivation was fairly obvious.

Leo, the guy who got me onto the set, told me the entire budget was under $50,000 and the video and Internet rights would yield more than $600,000 for the producer in one year. Not a bad return for three days of work. In the next issue, I will have an interview with Candice, one of the stars of the movie.

Bizarrely,
Lewis

❖❖❖

Greetings Fellow Bizarros:

As promised, today we have the much-anticipated interview with "Candice", the porn actress. What follows will probably surprise you, as it did me when interviewing her. Candice is a 22-year-old former hooker who has a college degree in psychology.

She is seemingly intelligent, definitely articulate and although beautiful and young, she appears older than her years. She takes no drugs. So many of the stereotypes I had in mind were shattered. The only one that remained and corroborated was that she is bi-sexual, but preferred women lovers. As luck would have it, this did not disturb me at all.

Without further rambling, here is the interview:

Lewis: Candice, how long have you been in the porn industry?

Candice: I started when I was 17. Oh, am I supposed to say that? I have been on my own since I was that age, and I made enough money to get through Junior College and the University of Illinois.

Lewis: What got you started?

Candice: I was on my own and became a lady of the evening initially. This was not a good time in my life, but one of my customers turned out to be a producer of porn films and asked me if I would like to become a star.

Lewis: Did you continue your other profession?

Candice: No, this was a way to stop turning tricks. That was a scary time in my life because you never knew what kind of people you would be sleeping with. In a film, you get to know the people and once you get over the fact that someone is shining a light up your ass, it gets easy.

Lewis: What is the hardest thing about acting in porn films?

Candice: It's usually not some guy's pecker (laughter...). Actually, it is the boredom that really gets to me. I mean how many times can you do the same thing over and over without getting bored?

Lewis: I saw you on the set and you did not look bored to me.

Candice: That is why it is called ACTING.

Lewis: Just one last question...being a sex symbol and the object of countless fantasies must be a hard thing to deal with on a personal level. How does your adult film career affect your personal life?

Candice: Well, it's not easy to keep a relationship going. When all you do at work is f***, sex is no longer the most important thing in your personal life. I'm really just like any other woman. I want romance and affection. Just because I work in the adult industry doesn't mean

I'm going to do you in the first five minutes. But if we do make an emotional connection I'll show you things no other woman can.

Well folks, that seemed like the best place to close the interview.

Bizarrely,
Lewis

❖❖❖

Greetings Fellow Bizarros:

I read a lot of newspapers. In fact I get them delivered from all over the country, looking for those perfect stories to include in Bizarre News. Occasionally I write a column about a story. Today is one of those times. This story does not come from Alabama. It comes from Tacoma, Washington.

Jake Hansen, a forty-two-year-old construction worker, was driving down a crowded street when he crashed into a parked car along the side of the street. There were two people inside getting ready to drive off. Jake had his pants unbuckled and was semi-conscious when the police arrived on the scene. I know, you are wondering what was he doing with his pants unbuckled.

When Jake came to his senses, he explained that he was trying to rub some anti-itch cream on his groin when he lost control of the wheel. The people who were in the parked car were not amused and when they got out of the hospital (with minor injuries) they sued Jake. Jock itch can be more hazardous than you think.

Here is the bizarre part. Jake is suing the company that puts out the cream because he maintains he was simply following directions. He maintains that there was not a statement on the label that gave suffi-cient warning as to the dangers of applying the cream to the groin area.

For all of you readers who do not live in the U.S., do we have a great country or what? WARNING: Do NOT read Bizarre News while driving. Bizarre News has been known to create a severe condition similar to convulsive states.

Bizarrely,
Lewis

❖❖❖

Greetings Fellow Bizarros:

A very bizarre story is circulating. I have heard about it for months and while I cannot guarantee its authenticity, I just had to pass this on. It seems that in Vatican City, a boy has been born with horns and a tail. Could this be the devil incarnate?

Church officials have been trying to keep this under wraps since September of last year, but I personally have heard it several times. A writer of the not-so-reputable "Weekly World News" tabloid contacted me two months ago and suggested that I check into this story. I did not, because it seemed too ridiculous to put on my Kolchak hat and look for Beelzebub.

But a reader sent me an article in Italian from the Vatican, and Paulie, our Ethnic Jokes editor, translated it for me. It was about this baby with horns being nursed by three separate wet nurses. The infant had horns and a tail. I did not believe the story, but decided to contact a local Priest of a Catholic church. Father "John" became nervous and directed me to another Priest who spoke to me on the condition of remaining anonymous.

The story gets even more bizarre as this Priest spoke to me in hushed tones telling me that he has heard that this story was real, although he had no first hand knowledge. The Vatican had tried to keep this story quiet as to not create a panic that the Devil had come into the world.

I asked the Father if he had a drug problem, which he certainly did not appreciate. It seems that there are some very mystical wings within the Catholic Church that most people do not know. There are special Priests that investigate miracles, others that do exorcisms, and still others that look for the Devil.

I would love to visit the Vatican to find out for myself, but I have to stick around the office and the boss would certainly frown on a business expense to look for the Devil. Well folks, this issue is another tour de force. Jane is really helping me find some of the most bizarre stuff around, and I am a little more free to do investigative work. Stay tuned!

Bizarrely,
Lewis

❖❖❖

Greetings fellow Bizarros:

There is a lot of talk in the U.S. about different versions of tax cuts. One idea is to eliminate "estate taxes". These are the taxes on your "estate" after you die. I started thinking about this issue in a deep mode until I discovered that I really didn't have an estate. Secondly, after I die I am more interested in what's on the other side than what I am leaving behind.

Then a reader tipped me off to a story that fit in with my musings. I followed up on it. In Cape Town, South Africa, an aging heiress by the name of Patricia O'Neill has cut off her husband from her will. This sort of stuff happens all the time, but the bizarre part is that she is leaving the equivalent of almost $60 million to her pet chimpanzee!

No kidding. Frank O'Neill, her out-in-the-cold husband is distraught and I managed to get a hold of him through the helpful digging of Jane. Below is a paraphrased short interview I had with Frank. I told him I was a reporter for *The Chicago Daily Herald.* (There is no such publication. I didn't think he would agree to an interview with Bizarre News.) So, journalistic ethics aside, here it is:

Lewis: Mr. O'Neill, news has crossed over 10,000 miles about your wife leaving her fortune to a chimpanzee. How does that make you feel?

Frank: Two things. First, I might not outlive my wife. So who cares? The second thing is I GUARANTEE I will outlive that disgusting chimp. You know chimps have accidents too.

Lewis: I believe the chimp's name is Kalu. Why did your wife see fit to do this?

Frank: Well, she is awfully fond of the bugger. Secondly, she pitched a fit on me when I left for the Sydney Olympics without taking her with me. Vengeance has no wrath you know.

Lewis: Does it bother you that this has become a public flap?

Frank: Actually, I am enjoying the opportunity of telling my side of the story. Kalu had already taken my place in many ways. Patricia is more fond of that hairy animal than me. I hated Kalu long before being cut out of the will. He was always smoking my cigars and one day I actually caught him wearing my under garments.

Lewis: We seem to be getting into some strange territory. You sound strangely jealous of Kalu.

The interview ended rather abruptly. Anyway, thanks to Jane for tracking Frank down. She's a bloodhound if there ever was one. Now, on to what you need, a fix of all the news that is not fit to print anywhere else!

Bizarrely,
Lewis

❖❖❖

Greetings Fellow Bizarros:

Several months back I told you a story about TZ and I heading to a strip club in Harvey, Illinois, called the "Sky Box." It is the only all-nude joint in the south suburbs. Naturally, we did this for research and not any prurient interest. Well, this refuge for the discriminating entertainment seeker is in the news this week.

It seems that a man was getting a table dance and he leaned back and burned himself when a candle on the table caught his shirt on fire. This is not the bizarre part. He is suing the establishment. Below are three parts of the complaint:

"[Skybox] negligently and carelessly allowed open candles on the tables to be used for lighting, when they knew or should have known that customers would be endangered by dancers embracing and dancing in close proximity to customers."

"[Skybox] negligently and carelessly failed to train its dancers so as to prevent this type of occurrence."

"[Skybox] negligently and carelessly failed to adequately screen or enclose the candle flame so as to prevent this type of occurrence."

The man's name is Alan Garner and he gets my vote for jackass-of-the-month. Why? He doesn't want to accept the responsibility of his search for a hot time turning into a "hot time." He further stated that the burns he received could permanently affect his sexual urges and that $50,000 was the least he would take to settle the lawsuit.

Now, is it me or is the judicial system completely goofed? That leads me to another story about a judge in Los Angeles named Patrick Murphy. He testified at a disciplinary hearing last week because he missed more than 400 workdays in recent years because he has a phobia about being a judge. Judge Patrick B. Murphy said, "I was disabled by this phobia. I was disabled by the bench."

I don't know, but these stories do not make me feel warm and fuzzy about the judicial system. On that note, we have a great issue (as always) for you and your friends to pass around. Remember to brighten someone else's day by sharing Bizarre News. Forward your copy to some unsuspecting Internet buddy today.

Bizarrely,
Lewis

❖❖❖

< < < < A Bizarre News Late-Breaking Issue > > > >

Man, I am dictating this issue to Jane on my cell phone. I am on the Dan Ryan and traffic is backed up behind me as far as the eye can see. About 2-3,000 feet ahead of me is a barricade of police cars across all the lanes. I got out of my car and walked forward a bit to see what the hell was going on and there is a nut in the middle of the expressway. It looks like he is waving around what may be a gun.

He is wearing a Coca Cola uniform and he has a Coca Cola van behind him. I have no idea why he is waving a gun, but a few of the people like me who got out of their cars suggested that he was going to kill himself. I hate to sound like a cold-hearted bastard, but if he wants to kill himself, I hope he does it before someone ELSE gets hurt.

The intrepid reporter that I am, I tried to get closer only to have one of Chicago's finest yell at me to get back in my vehicle. Here I am, Friday at 3:00 and I am stuck in a sea of cars. I have the radio on, but I do not know where they are getting their information. They say "negotiators" are on their way. I would prefer a sniper or two. According to the radio, the gunman has so far made no official demands.

I am telling you, I have moved back to about 1,000 feet, and I am wondering what is the range of his gun. At this point, as far as I can tell, he has re-entered his vehicle.

I do not know how this stuff happens to me, but it looks like I will be here for at least a few hours. Jane will be putting together the rest of Bizarre News because I don't think I will be getting back to the office tonight.

Bizarrely,
Lewis

❖❖❖

Greetings Fellow Bizarros:

Well, after several months of asking the boss to approve expenses for me to call a 900 number, I did it. I finally answered an ad that was emailed to me (ever since I answered the Penis enlargement ad, I get all kinds of weird ads.) The ad said:

Phone Dating, Meet women to date or just have nasty phone sex!

The following was taped for accuracy.

Operator: Are you interested in phone sex or just want to meet some nice ladies?

Lewis: If I wanted to meet ladies, I would hang out at the grocery store. Introduce me to some lesbian operators!

Operator: Hold on...

Operator #2: Hi, I am Lola and I am here to make your fantasy come true. Have you ever been in a hot threesome?

Lewis: Well, one time I made love to my wife with the cat at the foot of the bed. Does that count?

Operator #2: It depends on what the cat was doing while you were making love. But enough of your home life. I can tell you love to have a good time. What if I got Deloris to come on the phone with me. Then the three of us could have a reeeel good time.

[Folks...this was obviously a ploy to keep me on the phone. At $3.99 a minute, they had plenty of incentive. Anyway, I was getting rather aroused at the thought of Deloris and Lola on the other end.]

Lewis: What are the plans for the three of us? Get Deloris. Let's party!

Lola: So, what's your name and how do you like it?

Lewis: My name is...hmmm...Jake. They call me Jake the snake. [You don't think I would give 'em my real name?]

Deloris entering the call: How BIG is your snake? I had a snake once ...[censored.]

Lewis: Lola and Deloris, does your mother know what you ladies do?

The rest of the call highlights will be in the next issue.

Bizarrely,
Lewis

❖❖❖

Greetings Fellow Bizarros:

Today we have the second part of the 900 call to the sexy (at least they sounded that way) duo of Deloris and Lola. We received many emails asking that we leave the smut to that "low-life TZ", but we pursue all bounds of bad taste.

So, if you are easily offended, you have one of several choices. The two most obvious are skip this column today and go straight to the stories, or hit the delete button before you read any further!

For those of you still with us, here goes as sanitized as I possibly can make it:

Lewis: Hey, are the two of you in the same room?

Deloris: Would you like us to be? I wish you were here right now with us and we could show you just how close we really are.

[My mind was racing with the possibilities. I had suspended all disbelief for a short time. Upon reflection, there was probably only one fat lady in curlers speaking from home trying to paint her toenails. But this commentary is reflective. Old Lewis was getting turned on at the time!]

Lewis: This is my first time with phone sex. Am I supposed to do something while talking to you?

Deloris: Jake [I had almost forgotten I told her that was my name], do you have any oil or cream and a towel?

Lewis: Hold on here babe, I think I know where you are headed. I don't feel like polishing the wood. I'd rather hear what you and your friend do to each other inbetween calls.

Deloris: The first thing I love to do...is with my tongue, I like to lick [censored...] then take my fingers and slide them [censored...] She likes it when I use my [censored...] And then she uses it on me. By that time our [censored...] are so soaked it's hard to tell whose is whose.

Lola: Oh, yeah Deloris, you nasty little [censored...] Get on my [censored...] Mmmmm...Do it [censored...] harder on my [censored...]

Folks, Deloris and Lola kept me on the phone for a total of 17 minutes. Most of the conversation is simply not fit to print here. Our chief editor simply would not let me print the full transcript.

Speaking of the chief editor, he will be representing Bizarre News on the Sally Jesse Raphael show. They asked for me to appear, but I declined due to my undercover responsibilities. Check him out. He may not be as familiar with the mechanics of "bizarre" as much as I am, but he is still an entertaining guy. We chose the top five Bizarre News stories over the last four years, so find Sally on the dial and tune in.

Bizarrely,
Lewis

❖❖❖

Greetings Fellow Bizarros:

Well, I finally had an escape weekend with the wife. We went to beautiful downtown Chicago for a great time, except she dragged me to The

Chicago Art Museum. I felt like Aster's horse. For the young ones out there, Aster was this guy who always dressed his horse up to go to "Sunday Meeting". The horse looked good...but it was still a horse.

Any long time readers know that I am not exactly a connoisseur of the finer things in life. My idea of "class" is a stripper who showers. But the little lady wanted to go and she has put up with a lot of my unusual work responsibilities, so I quickly acquiesced. We spent about three hours roaming the labyrinth. Somehow, we got stuck in the section called "Contemporary Art."

If you know nothing about art (like me), this is the last place you want to be. I chanced upon one of the ugliest paintings I have ever seen. Before seeing the artist's name, I turned to my wife and said, "Honey, look at what someone passes off as art. The painter apparently only had blue paint and must have been depressed as Hell." The wife looked at me disgustedly and said, "Lewis, that's a Picasso. It's famous and called 'Old Man Playing Guitar' [as I recall]. Haven't you ever heard of Picasso's 'Blue Period?'"

It still looked like crap to me. It was Saturday and there were a lot of tour groups running around. The paranoid in me felt like they were following us around. Most of what I saw I didn't understand. It did not take long before I started getting annoyed. At one point I was looking at this painting and yelled at my wife [who was standing behind me], "Why is THIS art? It looks like someone tied a paint brush to a gerbil's tail and let it roam all over the canvass." I discovered that this was a Jackson Pollack.

Apparently I was kind of loud and this tour group erupted into laughter. I walked to the guard and asked how we could get out of this contemporary art section. She asked, "Where do you want to go?" My wife, deeply embarrassed by now cut in and said, "Anywhere but here. My husband is artistically challenged."

We left and went to the Cheesecake Factory. The world became right once again!

Bizarrely,
Lewis

❖❖❖

Greetings Fellow Bizarros:

I am sending this issue from some secluded place in Wisconsin. I am on assignment, and this is positively the scariest assignment I have ever been on. But I am ahead of the story. My latest adventure began last Wednesday evening when I was at a local gin mill, relaxing and decompressing from a tough day at the office. The bar was crowded when the TV flashed a picture of Timothy McVeigh. The guy sitting next to me muttered under his breath, "There is an American hero."

Most of the time I would simply ignore such a statement, but something inside me pushed me to start a conversation. He wasn't drunk, but he had obviously been drinking a while. He was prematurely balding with his hair buzzed high and tight. He reminded me of the actor Ed Harris. He called himself JR. He was in a Wisconsin militia group that idolized the nut case McVeigh. I told him that I was a journalist and asked if I could interview him for this column.

I had never met someone who had admitted being in a militia. JR seemed rather normal but was paranoid. I did not expect him to agree to the interview, but he started rambling on and on about how the U.S. government was slowly taking away the rights of the people. He felt that guys like McVeigh were heroes for fighting back against the system. He seemed unconcerned that over 140 women and children were killed in the Oklahoma bombing.

I am not sure why this guy was talking to me, for all he knew, I could have been lying and been an FBI man. JR continued to rail against U.S. institutions. He spent a lot of time on the IRS (this actually sounded pretty good to me). I did not know much about the politics of Waco, Randy Wheeler, and a lot of stuff JR was talking about, and I will not bore you with the details. But what was emerging for me was a picture of a dangerous group of guys who like to play war.

These militiamen think they are the spiritual heirs to Sam Adams and The Boston Tea Party crowd. After about an hour and a half, JR asked me if I wanted to do some "real reporting" and come with him to a training exercise in Wisconsin. I have NO FRICKIN' idea why I said yes. That is why I am in some God-forsaken place. I will fill you in on what is going on later.

Bizarrely
Lewis

❖❖❖

Greetings Fellow Bizarros:

One of my co-workers at an editorial meeting about a month ago suggested a column about the "Swinging Lifestyle." I briefly mentioned this story idea to my wife and before I could even tell her this was JUST A STORY IDEA, she instantly told me that she would have no part of this. Honey, relax. I am a reporter!

I am an admitted square. Writing Bizarre News is a vicarious thrill; anything goes inside this publication. I am more content to chronicle instead of participate. (Okay, I did go to a nudist colony, but I carried my laptop EVERYWHERE.) In any case, I was watching this show on HBO called "Real Sex" and they had a segment in between teaching men cunnilingus and rubber dolls. The segment was on "swinging."

I took this as a sign, so I hopped on the Internet and came across this place in Florida called "The Trapeze Club." I asked the proprietor if I could get a hold of a couple. He gave me the email address (sorry folks, it is confidential) of Mr. and Ms. Trapeze who act as sort of ambassadors for the lifestyle.

I contacted them. What a surprise. I thought it would be like speaking to a sleaze-bag couple, you know, the kind you used to meet at a bar right before last call?

They were both articulate. I asked "Mr. Trapeze" how he could handle his wife smoking someone else's bologna. He was not amused by the colorful term. (Thanks to TZ at Laff A Day for that one.) I visited Ms. Trapeze's website and thought she was gorgeous.

I asked why she was into this kind of lifestyle. She said, "I am trying to educate people that alternatives in physical pleasure are multi-dimensional. I want to bring CLASS to this swinging lifestyle and represent it with dignity." This couple goes to the club often. But only on the weekends because she teaches a class during the week. I guess she only goes to the club when she has no class.

Most males believe we are genetically predisposed to have multiple partners. But most guys I know would be ticked to have the love of their life grinding in an orgy room with a dentist. But what do I know?

Bizarrely,
Lewis

Greetings Fellow Bizarros:

I was at the airport the other day when I saw this couple that had piercings all over their body, or at least the parts that I could see. They looked like human pin cushions. I am the first to admit that I know next to nothing why someone wants to look like a human zipper, so I decided to do some research.

The term body piercing is fairly self-evident. It refers to the piercing of the body with a hollow gauge needle and the installation of surgical grade steel (or gold, titanium, surgical plastic) jewelry into the tongue, nipples, nostril, naval, lips, labia, eyebrow, ear cartilage, ear lobe, perineum, penis, scrotum, septum, clitoral hood and clitoris proper (if I have left out any body part, please do not drop me a line about it.)

I discovered that a common and enduring theme is the impact that piercing the body has on both an individual's self identity and feelings of group affiliation. When I was growing up, tie-dying was the less painful alternative.

I met a couple of people who do the piercing for a living - "Bill" and "George." These guys weigh a few pounds more themselves from the needles and chains they connect.

Bill and George (and Louise to a lesser extent) are visibly heavily pierced. In their roles as proprietors of the two professional piercing studios they act as evangelists of the practice. If they had their way, every new-born male would be pierced instead of circumcised. I asked why this was so popular. He had one word - SEX.

Piercing the body to heighten the experience of sex is a common theme and popular interest in the practice is often the way in which piercing services are 'sold' to the public. I asked if this was really the case and they offered to pierce my nipple for free.

I suggested that I would rather be tortured by the KGB than undergo sticking something sharp through my nipple. They were not amused. They cut short my interview, leaving me with only a glimmer of an idea as to why parents would let their children mutilate themselves.

Bizarrely,
Lewis

❖❖❖

Greetings Fellow Bizarros:

I am an admitted conspiracy nut. I read books like *Gideon's Spies* (on Israeli intelligence activities throughout the world), UFO conspiracies, cattle mutilations, crop circles...you name it, I read about it. It is not that I am more gullible then the next guy, I just think this stuff is interesting, even though most of it is garbage.

I started to think about which "conspiracy" really grabbed attention and then later was discovered to be a hoax. I ran across The Iron Mountain Report, which was first penned in 1967. This was supposedly a secret, U.S. government report that outlined why war was a GOOD thing. The gist of the document was that war created "vital social and economic controls."

For five years, this report circulated throughout the world. It was translated into 15 languages. There were other claims that really strained the imagination. Among them was the contention that pollution was a deliberate and needed to maintain birth control. Also, if peace broke out all over the world, it would be necessary to put drugs into the water supply to maintain control.

Then in 1972, the author of the "secret" report, Leonard Lewin, admitted that he wrote it to see how gullible people were to conspiracies. I was not "really" duped, although I still am wondering what happened to my cat 15 years ago. I still think an alien abducted him.

Bizarrely,
Lewis

❖❖❖

Greetings Fellow Bizarros:

I was doing research for an issue regarding weird cults. Writing about cattle mutilations will do that to you. As is the case with research, you start on one thing and pretty soon you are far a field. I learned about some weird cult in India called "Thugee." This was a secret society devoted to the Hindu goddess called Kali, goddess of death and destruction.

At first glance they were just your average, underground, Hindu death cult. But the plot begins to thicken because this Thugee cult kept records (so the British Raj claimed) of their deeds. It seems that for over three hundred years, its members had a ritual of strangling folks. From 1550 to 1850 its records indicated the Thugee cult strangled 2,000,000 people in India alone...at least according to British government files put in evidence at a trial in the 19th Century. It almost makes me want to introduce my mother-in-law to a Thugee or is it a Thuger?

The British were the colonial power in India for years and they had plenty of their people strangled by the Thugee cult. They brought 4,000 cult members to trial. It was at this trial that a British prosecutor brought evidence claiming two million murders. ALL four thousand Thugees were hanged by the British. Now, 150 years later, the cult is being rehabilitated by revisionist historians. It seems that the British "slightly" exaggerated the number of strangulations to stir up public appetites so the mass executions could take place. Estimates of the cult's deeds range toward 20,000 over 300 years. Anyone want to visit Bombay?

Bizarrely,
Lewis

Greetings Fellow Bizarros:

I have a question for you. How much would YOU pay for Napoleon Bonaparte's penis? This is no idle question because once upon a time in 1972, someone tried to sell it. No kidding! Before eBay ever tried to sell a kidney, the Christie's auction house tried selling Napoleon's dick.

It seems that for some unexplained reason, when good old Napoleon died he had an autopsy. A physician in attendance decided to keep a memento and sliced his manhood, put it in a jar, and for generations, passed it on to his heirs. I bet the readings of the wills were interesting, "...and to my daughter Monique, I bequeath Napoleon's penis..."

But Napoleon's manhood did not hit the minimum bid to be sold and was taken off the market. Nobody even bid $2,500 for this piece of history. In 1977 an American Urologist purchased what was left of the penis for $3,800. Now I know many of you want to know what the size of the penis was. One inch! A measly one inch (that's 2.54 centimeters ...which makes it sound bigger.) The water in the storage jar must have been cold.

Now there are other bits of famous people that have been sold at auction. Sotheby's in London auctioned a four-inch lock of Beethoven's hair in 1994. The purchaser paid $,9000 and he wanted to do DNA testing to prove the rumors that Beethoven had African blood in him.

Anyway, this seems like a good place to start when you are trying to figure out what you are worth.

Bizarrely,

Lewis

❖❖❖

Greetings fellow Bizarros:

Life around here gets rather weird. We have a lot of fun around here, but the CEO is forever trying to get inter-departmental harmony. How does he do this? Well, one time he invited me into the advertising sales department for my input. This was a disaster that to this day brings groans from the crew.

The latest foray for me was to be in a merchandising meeting. You know when the ad sales department doesn't sell ad space, we use the space to sell everything from breast cream to diet pills. The boss wanted MY input on future products. The older I get, the more convinced I am that I know so little. What is going to sell is just one more area to display my lack of knowledge.

One product that was brought up to discuss was called "The Travel Mate." This is a camping product for women. It is a tube that is "inserted" into a woman's "female anatomy" (that is what the brochure actually says) so ladies never again have to sit on unsanitary areas to urinate. In other words, they no longer have to squat to piss!

This plastic utensil actually looks like the dispenser for liquid medicine that children use. Here are the ACTUAL SELLING POINTS the company touts:

· Six-inch Travel Mate is small enough to fit in your pocket or purse
· Cradle forms liquid tight seal for female anatomy
· Travel Mate was inspired by a fire hose nozzle

Just so you know, I did not vote to test this product. But the weird thing was that three women asked for a sample. Hmmmm!

Bizarrely,
Lewis

❖❖❖

Greetings Fellow Bizarros:

I know absolutely nothing about the military except that it is the last place I want to be when a war starts. Being a coward is not a great qualification for carrying a gun. But there is so much talk about a missile defense program that will shoot down incoming warheads that I wanted to do some research into this.

The idea seems a bit crazy to me. In the Gulf War, I found out that not a single missile was intercepted in mid air. Several incoming Iraqi SCUD missiles simply blew up in the air on their own. I think they must have been Chinese missiles.

In any case, I wanted to know who these "experts" were that advocated spending billions of dollars on this defense system. It is not surprising to find out that General Dynamics, Raytheon and Hughes Electronics are all for it. But who were the experts? Here is where it gets bizarre. A leading missile expert and advisor to the Pentagon just happens to be Jeff "Skunk" Baxter from the Doobie Brothers. Baxter plays guitar and in his spare time is an amateur missile defense expert.

Now, this is CRAZY. Our top military brass gets advice from a drug addled, aging rock star. This may be the most incredible thing I have heard since a woman came home one night without her panties and told her husband that an alien abducted her and took her undergarments. I think his name was Juan.

I wonder what is next. Last week I found out that New Zealand wanted to tax cow farts and this week I learned that "Star Wars" was being promoted by the "Skunk." I love my job!

Bizarrely,
Lewis

❖❖❖

Greetings Fellow Bizarros:

So many of the emails I have been receiving lately revolve around the "Monkey Man" in India. For new subscribers, there is mass hysteria over a supposed half-man, half-monkey creature terrorizing India. My first thoughts stemmed from Western chauvinism. I chalked up the reports to uneducated Indians in some mass delusion.

I started thinking, "How does such a crock of crap take hold?" But in the good old U.S. of A, we have our own mass delusions. We have Sasquatch (or Bigfoot). I first thought Sasquatch was a former Chicago Bull by the name of Will Perdue, but that is another column. We have the mass delusions of alien abductions and angel sightings. The Irish have Leprechauns. I am not sure where the Loch Ness monster is (accept it is in Loch Ness, Scotland).

But the Monkey Man mystery is special. I have my own theories. I communicated with a New Delhi witness by email who supposedly saw this creature. He told me the creature was more man than monkey and very strong. He saw him hop from one building to another.

A detailed description that he gave to me was VERY strange. The more detail that I read, the more clear the picture in my mind became. The picture he described actually sounded like TZ, our editor of Laff A Day. I will bet you that the Monkey Man and TZ have never been seen in the same room at the same time. In any case, we have one great issue lined up. Other people took the weekend off, but I was researching stories for this issue. Hope you enjoy.

Bizarrely,
Lewis

❖❖❖

Greetings Fellow Bizarros:

My oldest son (now 12) finished school and was showing me all of the essays he had written. There was one about me and Bizarre News that I thought I would share:

"My Father" - By Eddie

Having a Dad like mine is strange. I am constantly wishing for a normal one like you sometimes see on TV. A few months ago he gave me a copy of his book, *The Best of Bizarre News* and I got a chance to see what he does for a job. When he gave me the book, he said, "Son, you are now a man." Gee, thanks, Dad.

I can't tell all of my friends that my father interviews prostitutes at brothels. I just learned what those things were. So I told my friends that my Dad was a fireman. I mean one day he came home from a business trip and I was helping Mom unload his suitcase. His shirt had bloodstains on it and there were feathers stuck in the sleeves. I remember at the time being worried that he got hurt and asked Mom. She said, "Never mind, your father is fine."

It was not until I read the book that I found out that my father was at a live cockfight in Phoenix, Arizona. I once mentioned this to a friend and his mother overheard. From that point, she would never let us be in the same room alone because she thought that I must be weird like my dad. That is why I now say he is a fireman.

But there are some cool things about being his son. He thinks grades are not that important because they don't really matter that much. As long as you try, you can be whatever you want to be in life. I thought about it. Would I want to be like my Dad? The answer is I would not mind seeing what a brothel looks like.

Eddie

It looks like my kid is a chip off the old block! Now his mother isn't exactly thrilled at the prospects of Eddie becoming a chronicler of the weird. In any case, we have a super issue lined up today, so grab a cup of coffee and relax.

Bizarrely,
Lewis

❖❖❖

Greetings Fellow Bizarros:

As many of you know, we operate in the south suburbs of Chicago. There will be big things happening here soon. TZ tipped me off to a convention of Swamis coming to town in June. I am trying to get press credentials to allow me to cover this unprecedented event.

For those who do not know, "Swami" is a title of respect for Hindu spiritual guides, kind of like the word "Reverend." Except these guys hang out in orange diapers. My interests in Swamis is no doubt in part colored by me learning meditation several years ago at the Maharishi University in Fairfield, Iowa. My instructor was a great guy and I have been free of ulcers ever since, but he was not a Swami.

I never learned "advanced techniques" beyond the meditation exercises. They had a course to teach you how to levitate. The cost was only $1,500. For some strange reason, I never have believed in this practice. Maybe I can take one of our Mekai cameras to snap a few shots of a Swami levitating.

But a convention of Swamis coming to Chicago seems like fertile ground for bizarreness. Why Chicago? Well, this town has become sort of a religious pilgrimage for Swamis I was told by a monk I once met.

Have you ever had a conversation with an honest-to-goodness Swami? I wonder what it takes to become one. Do you go to Swami school? Do you get a Swami certificate? Here in the U.S., 3,000 people put on their tax forms that they were "Santa Claus" for a living. Imagine filling out an IRS form and putting "Swami" for your occupation. An audit is highly likely.

I know that it may seem politically incorrect, but I can't help but think of the Three Stooges doing their Swami routine whenever hearing the word "Swami". I will keep you updated if I can get in. Any suggestions from Indians on how I might blend in? Anyway, we have a great issue for you so sit back, relax and levitate if you have a mind to.

Bizarrely,
Lewis

Greetings Fellow Bizarros:

Has anyone seen the recent study out of one of our finest institutions, Wake Forest? This university got psychologists, psychiatrists and physicists together to study the "Alien Abduction" phenomena (I guess you needed to be a "P" profession.) Together, they identified several "signs" for people who believe they were abducted.

I will not list all of them, but the top five signs indicating whether you were abducted or not included:

* You experience an unexplained nausea or strange sense of uneasiness around the same time of the day.
[Heck, you might also be pregnant.]

* You have an unusual new scar or strange mark on your body.
[Especially if you had a lot to drink the night before!]

* You often find yourself hungry for oranges and lemons.
[I think scurvy would be a better guess.]

* You have a strong feeling that you were meant to do something special in life.
[This is also known as ambition.]

* You often find yourself rummaging through your trash as well as other people's trash.

If anyone has exhibited all of these signs then they were most likely abducted by aliens. If you only like rummaging through trash, you are simply sick. I am glad I read about this study because we have been eliminating potential colleges for where I want my sons to go...and Wake Forest has now made the list.

Bizarrely,
Lewis

Greetings Fellow Bizarros:

I am in the land of the "Mouse" in Orlando with the family. Jane is doing the stories and all I have to do is this column and the reader comments. Thanks, Jane! The last time we were here some nut stayed in Sea World after closing and swam with the killer whales and was killed. His family sued Sea World for not giving appropriate warning that killer whales were dangerous!

This was a last minute deal and my travel agent called and got a deal on a charter out of Midway Airport. After checking in the luggage at the curb, we proceeded to the gate. After a few minutes, I noticed that we were on the same charter as the musicians scheduled to play at Epcot. I felt like we were in a 21st century version of Soul Train - Soul Plane!

Our first park visit was to Magic Kingdom. Since I forgot my hat at home, and the weather was only slightly cooler than Hell, I needed to get a hat. I knew this trip was headed for bizarreness when I picked out a hat and my son Eddie and I approached the cashier. The cashier muttered something to me and I politely said, "I am sorry, but I do not speak Spanish."

Eddie immediately went to the shelf and got another hat, exactly like the one I brought to the counter, only this one had a price tag. The cashier rang up the hat and I walked out of the shop asking Eddie how he understood Spanish. Eddie looked at me and chuckled, "Dad, he wasn't speaking Spanish, he was just speaking English with an accent."

You gotta hand it to the Disney folks. They change rides to fit the times. In the Pirates of the Caribbean exhibit, the pirates are no longer chasing the fair maidens. The pirates are now being chased. When I asked an attendant what had happened to the exhibit he told me that pirates chasing women drew criticism from women's organizations. Apparently N.O.W. (National Organization for Women) complained that the old Pirates of the Caribbean promoted "rape" so they decided to have women chasing the pirates with pitchforks. This, of course, makes no sense whatsoever. So Disney is now no longer promoting rape, but the kids are coming off the rides totally confused.

Bizarrely,
Lewis

❖❖❖

Greetings Fellow Bizarros:

We used to have an advertiser that sold this stuff called "GroBust". It was a cream that when liberally applied, supposedly made your breasts grow. The advertiser complained "the ad didn't work" and I suggested the salesman tell them it probably worked better than the product.

So when I saw this story inside the *New Scientist* (heck, I spend all of my time reading) I began to wonder. It seems that research in Australia has finally come up with something good. You can now "grow your own breasts." Tissue engineer Kevin Cronin has developed a technique to grow breast cells. Rather than growing breast cells in the lab and then transplanting it back into the body, Cronin grows the tissue directly on a woman's body.

It is thought that this will soon replace silicon breast implants. Now, he is not telling the scientific community exactly how he is doing this because he has applied for a patent. But he insists that this will have many other applications as well, including the buttocks and facial areas.

I wonder if you grow tissue from the buttocks on facial areas if you would then be called "Ass-face." Come to think about it, I think I dated a girl who had this done to her years ago. Cronin swears his research has been completely successful on mice claiming he has grown quite a rack on several subjects. Rumor has it Disney is lining up Minnie for the next trials.

Bizarrely,
Lewis

❖❖❖

Greetings Fellow Bizarros:

We get a lot of email around here. EVERY piece of email gets read, and occasionally it even gets an action! A reader named Horst sent me information on insurance. I really do not like even speaking about insurance, but I decided to do some research on a particular kind of insurance.

Did you know that you could ACTUALLY get insurance against being abducted by aliens? No kidding. And the best thing about this policy is that it is cheap. For $19.95 plus $3 for shipping you the policy, you get a $10 million policy. Below is an ad I found:

Don't Leave Earth Without It

Agents are standing BY...We accept all pre-existing conditions. You can't be turned down regardless of age.

You can purchase this Policy for anyone (who qualifies), such as your spouse or even your mother-in-law, and yes, name yourself as the Beneficiary!

Single Lifetime Premium $19.95 + $3.00 Same Day Shipping

Each Personalized Gold Bordered Policy includes a "Frequent Flyer Endorsement" and a Claim Form, which requires the signature of an Authorized Onboard Alien.

Every time I write about alien abductions, we get several traumatized people who claim they have been abducted. Now, for just under $23 bucks you can have a $10 million policy. If you are going to be abducted, you might as well get rich.

Anyway, we have a great issue and some exciting things on the horizon. Stay tuned as Bizarre News covers all the news that others dare not touch!

Bizarrely,
Lewis

8

Oddities & Absurdities

Sometimes the things people say can be just as bizarre as the things people do. And sometimes they can be just plain funny. Bizarre News readers have been extremely generous in sending me stories, lists, quotes and various oddities. Many of them I print in the email edition, and the best of those I have collected for you here. While the following pages include a few lists of bizarre facts I have tried to steer more towards the humorous end of the spectrum. Humor is an important part of Bizarre News, because it's just not emotionally healthy to read every issue with a shocked look on your face.

Bizarre Revenge

After his wife left him, spurned husband Donald Niblett wrecked their home with a bulldozer, causing damage in excess of 15,000 English pounds.

In 1988, an Egyptian belly-dancer paid back her unfaithful husband by going on a massive spending spree with his credit card totalling $46,000 before flying to his villa in France and smashing the place up.

A married pilot dismissed his mistress from his London apartment. The young woman agreed to leave but asked for a day to pack her belongings. When he returned from an overseas flight he found the phone off the hook. His mistress had made a long distance call to the speaking clock in Washington D.C.

A housewife, distraught over her husband's unfaithfulness, decided to throw herself out of the window of their third floor apartment. She didn't realize her husband was walking beneath. She survived, he did not.

❖❖❖

Bizarre Lawsuits

A University of Idaho freshman suffered fractured vertebrae, abrasions and severely bruised buttocks when the dormitory window that he was mooning a group of friends through shattered. The young man and his parents sued the school for $470,000 per cheek.

When Minnesota State Bank of St. Paul president Michael Brennan flushed the toilet in the executive washroom, he was blasted with a geyser of 200 to 300 gallons of raw sewage. He sued the city and a construction company that neglected to inform anyone they shut off the sewer line for $50,000 to cover his humiliation and embarrassment.

A 25-year-old mortuary driver was cited for driving alone in a High Occupancy Vehicle lane. The man appeared in court and explained to the judge that he was transporting four dozen corpses at the time and wasn't alone. The judge didn't buy it and the mortuary driver was forced to pay a "stiff" fine.

A $35 million lawsuit was filed in New York State Supreme Court against Motorola. Ronald Silber claimed Motorola should be held liable for injuries they sustained when a car collided with them because the driver lost control of the car when reaching for her cell phone.

❖❖❖

Bizarre Premonitions

After having nightmares for ten consecutive nights about a DC-10 crash, Cincinnati office manager David Booth called American Airlines on May 22, 1979. Three days later, 273 people died when an American DC-10 crashed at Chicago.

In 1896, German psychic Madame de Ferriem had a vision of bodies being carried out of a coal mine at Dux in Bohmeia in bitterly cold weather. A year later hundreds were killed by an explosion in a coal mine in Dux during a cold spell.

"Fugitive" star David Jensen had a dream in 1980 where he saw himself being carried out in a coffin after a heart attack. His psychic's advice to go in for a physical came too late, for two days later Jensen died of a massive heart attack.

On the morning of April 14, 1965, Julia Grant, wife of U.S. General Ulysses S. Grant had a strong feeling that she and her husband should get out of Washington. As they were leaving, the couple passed John Wilkes Booth on his way to assasinate President Lincoln at the theatre. Grant was also found to be on Booth's death list.

Bizarre Political Insults

"He makes George Bush seem like a personality" - Jackie Mason on John Major.

"He is a sheep in sheep's clothing" - Winston Churchill on Clement Attlee.

"Winston, if I were your wife, I would put poison in your coffee." "Nancy, if I were your husband, I would drink it." - A conversation between Nancy Astor and Winston Churchill.

"He could not see a belt without hitting below it." - Margot Asquith on David Lloyd George.

"Richard Nixon impeached himself. He gave us Gerald Ford as his revenge." - U.S. politician Bella Abzug on Tricky Dickie.

"Nixon's motto was, 'If two wrongs don't make a right, try three." - U.S. writer Norman Cousins.

"Gerry Ford is so dumb that he can't fart and chew gum at the same time." - former U.S. President Lyndon B. Johnson.

"I wouldn't say she is open-minded on the Middle East, so much as empty-headed. She probably thinks Sinai is the plural of sinus." - Jonathan Aitken on Margaret Hatcher.

"Harry Truman proves that old adage that any man can become President of the United States." - U.S. politician Norman Thomas.

"A shiver looking for a spine to run up." - Harold Wilson on Edward Heath.

Bizarre Management Quotes

Recently, a magazine ran a contest. They were looking for people to submit quotes from their real-life managers. Here are some of the submissions:

As of tomorrow, employees will only be able to access the building using individual security cards. Pictures will be taken next Wednesday and employees will receive their cards in two weeks. (This was the winning quote from Fred Dales at Microsoft Corp in Redmond, Washington.)

E-mail is not to be used to pass on information or data. It should be used only for company business (Accounting manager, Electric Boat Company).

Doing it right is no excuse for not meeting the schedule. No one will believe you solved this problem in one day! We've been working on it for months. Now, go act busy for a few weeks and I'll let you know when it's time to tell them. (R&D supervisor, Minnesota Mining and Manufacturing/3M Corp.)

Quote from the Boss: "Teamwork is a lot of people doing what I say." (Marketing executive, Citrix Corporation).

We recently received a memo from senior management saying: "This is to inform you that a memo will be issued today regarding the subject mentioned above." (Microsoft, Legal Affairs Division).

One day my boss asked for a status report concerning a project I was working on. I asked him if tomorrow would be soon enough. He said "If I wanted it tomorrow, I would have waited until tomorrow to ask for it!" (New business manager, Hallmark Greeting Cards.)

Bizarre Foods

Perhaps one of life's most mysterious foods is SPAM. Here are some interesting facts that you may not have known about the "other" other white meat.

Spam stands for Shoulder, Pork and hAM.

It was launched by the Geo. A. Hormel Company of Austin, Minnesota, in 1937 and became a great favorite of military cooks during WWII because it contained protein, was easy to digest and convenient.

A six-year-old Dorset boy became addicted to Spam and ate his way through six tins of the stuff every week for three years. He had to be sent to a child psychiatrist to get him back on a normal diet.

Over four billion cans of Spam have been sold worldwide.

The Hormel Plant at Austin, Texas, contains an oven that cooks 450 cans of Spam a minute.

Spam came to Britain as part of the Lend Lease Act whereby food given to the U.K. would be paid for after the war. Often the only meat available, it became indispensable until rationing ended in 1954.

❖❖❖

Bizarre Con-Artists

In 1872, veteran prospectors Philip Arnold and John Slack bought $35,000 worth of diamonds in Europe and scattered them on land in Wyoming. They managed to convince the Bank of San Francisco they had discovered a diamond field and made $700,000.

Starting in 1921, Oscar Merril Hartzell began a scam selling fake shares in the estate of Sir Francis Drake. He contacted as many families as he could find with the surname Drake and was eventually accused of defrauding 270,000 people. The hoax netted him over $2,000,000.

When J. Bam Morrison arrived at Wetumka, Oklahoma, in 1950, he claimed to be the advance publicity man for Bohn's United Circus, which, he maintained, was due to hit town in three weeks. He allegedly sold advertising space to local traders...for a circus that didn't exist.

By forging signatures, James Addison Reavis was able to claim he was the legal owner of 17,000 square miles of Arizona. The enterprise raked in $300,000 a year until he was arrested in 1895 and sentenced to six years in prison.

Joseph Weill, who inspired the movie *The Sting*, rented abandoned banks and convinced businessmen that he had set up a genuine bank. He waited for them to deposit large sums of money before shutting down and moving on to the next town. This, plus some of his other scams, earned him over $6,000,000.

❖❖❖

Bizarre Insurance Claims

I thought my window was down but found it up when I put my head through it.

To avoid hitting the car bumper in front, I hit the pedestrian.

The pedestrian had no idea what direction to go, so I ran over him.

The guy was all over the road. I had to swerve a number of times before I hit him.

Bizarre Defense

In 1996, a Californian judge ruled against James Pflugradt's estate and in favor of the deceased's former landlord. The judge allowed the landlord to keep Pflugradt's $825 security deposit because he died without giving 30 days notice.

Troy Matthew Gentzler confessed to tossing rocks at cars from an overpass on Interstate 83 near York, Pennsylvania. But his lawyer claimed he was the victim of "Roid rage," erratic emotional swings caused by steroid use.

In October 1996, Charles S. Shapiro begged the Montgomery County, Maryland, court to allow him to change his plea to not guilty of hiring a hit man. He claimed his judgment had been impaired because he had ingested tranquilizers along with a bottle of Tums before confessing.

A Saint Louis, Missouri, man argued that the reason the jury found him guilty of stealing court documents wasn't that it had been prejudiced against him. The man claimed he was demonized because the judge allowed the jury to learn he was a lawyer.

❖❖❖

Bizarre Excuses for Missing School

[These are actual excuse notes from parents (including original spelling) from some schools in Texas.]

My son is under a doctor's care and should not take P.E. today. Please execute him.

Please excuse Gloria from Jim today. She is administrating.

Carlos was absent yesterday because he was playing football. He was hurt in the growing part.

Megan could not come to school today because she has been bothered by very close veins.

Please excuse Ray Friday from school. He has very loose vowels.

Please excuse Mary for being absent. She was in bed with gramps.

Please excuse Tommy for being absent yesterday. He had diarrhea and his boots leak.

❖❖❖

Bizarre Medical Records

This is an actual collection from medical interview records written by various paramedics, emergency room receptionists, and (we are afraid) a doctor or two at major hospitals...

She stated that she had been constipated for most of her life until 1989 when she got a divorce.

The patient was in his usual state of good health until his airplane ran out of gas and crashed.

Bleeding started in the rectal area and continued to Los Angeles.

Both breasts are equal and reactive to light and accommodation.

Exam of genitalia reveals that he is circus sized.

Exam of genitalia was completely negative except for the right foot.

The lab test indicated abnormal lover function.

The patient was to have a bowel resection. However he took a job as a stockbroker instead.

Bizarre Resumes

HOW NOT TO WRITE A RESUME. Bizarre News readers may have seen this list. These excerpts were compiled from actual resumes (not applicants to ShagMail, however) and have appeared in magazines and numerous online publications.

"Was met with a string of broken promises and lies, as well as cockroaches."

"Please call me after 5:30 because I am self-employed and my employer does not know I am looking for another job."

"I was proud to win the Gregg Typting Award."

"Physical disabilities include minor allergies to house cats and Mongolian sheep."

"Instrumental in ruining entire operation for Midwest chain operation."

"They insisted that all employees get to work by 8:45 every morning. Couldn't work under those conditions."

"I was working for my mom until she decided to move."

"Work Experience: Dealing with customer conflicts that arouse."

❖❖❖

Bizarre Authors' Names

These names are completely genuine and have been corroborated in the catalogues of the British Library and in the American National Union Catalog, as well as other authoritative sources.

Ole Bagger	Stanka Fuckar
Gottfried Egg	Dr F.P.H. Prick van Wily
Baron Filibarto Vagina d'Emarese	A. Schytte
Mme J.J. Fouqueau de Pussy	Simon Young-Suck Moon

❖❖❖

Bizarre Historical Misconceptions

There is no evidence that Betsy Ross sewed the first U.S. flag. The story didn't even flutter forth from her relatives until 1870.

George Washington did not toss a dollar across the Potomac. Even if he did toss something, the dollar didn't come into being until after the U.S. gained independence.

Francis Scott Key did not write our national anthem. He penned the words then set them to an old English drinking song. It did not become our national anthem until 1931.

Most of the midnight ride of Paul Revere was accomplished by other horsemen. It was Samuel Prescott, in fact, who carried the warning to Concord.

The Declaration of Independence was not approved on July 4, 1776. Only John Hancock, for the assembly, signed it that day. The other signatures were made on August 2.

George Washington wasn't the first U.S. President. John Hanson was the president of the Congress of the Confederation and carried the title of president of the U.S., as did eight men after him.

Bizarre Presidential Facts

Abraham Lincoln did not write the Gettysburg Address on the back of an envelope. In fact, he worked on that address for two weeks.

It was Cicero, not President John F. Kennedy, who first said words to the effect of, "Ask not what your country can do for you, but what you can do for your country."

Some scholars believe Andrew Jackson was born at sea in 1755, not 1767, and thus was not eligible to be president of the U.S. However, at least two states, North Carolina and South Carolina, claim his birth place, about a mile apart.

In 1824, Andrew Jackson received more popular votes than John Adams, yet lost the election. The vote was so close that neither candidate received a majority of the electoral votes. The decision then went to the House of Representatives, which elected Adams.

Zachary Taylor, twelfth president of the U.S., did not vote until he was sixty-two. He did not even vote in his own election.

President Ulysses S. Grant was once arrested during his term of office. He was convicted of exceeding the Washington speed limit on his horse and was fined $20.

❖❖❖

Bizarre Sexually Suggestive Town Names

Intercourse, Alabama

Clapper Gap, California

Climax, Colorado

Cumming, Georgia

Bald Knob, Arkansas

Rough and Ready, California

Blue Ball, Delaware

French Lick, Indiana

Beaver Lick, Kentucky	Eros, Louisiana
Assawoman Bay, Maryland	Gay Head, Massachusetts
Conception, Missouri	Square Butt, Montana
Horneytown, N. Carolina	Bowlegs, Oklahoma
Oral, S. Dakota	Humptulips, Washington

❖❖❖

Bizarre Sports Quotes

Chicago Cubs outfielder Andre Dawson on being a role model: "I want all the kids to do what I do, to look up to me. I want all the kids to copulate me."

And, upon hearing Joe Jacobi of the 'Skins say: "I'd run over my own mother to win the Super Bowl," Matt Millen of the Raiders said: "To win, I'd run over Joe's Mom, too."

Bill Peterson, a Florida State football coach: "You guys line up alphabetically by height." And "You guys pair up in groups of three, then line up in a circle."

Jim Finks, New Orleans Saints General Manager, when asked after a loss what he thought of the refs: "I'm not allowed to comment on lousy, no good officiating."

Lincoln Kennedy, Oakland Raiders tackle, on his decision not to vote: "I was going to write myself in, but I was afraid I'd get shot."

Torrin Polk, University of Houston receiver, on his coach, John Jenkins: "He treats us like men. He lets us wear earrings."

And the Gem: Oiler coach Bum Phillips when asked by Bob Costas why he takes his wife on all road trips, Phillips responded: "Because she is too damn ugly to kiss good-bye."

Bizarre Statements

These are from an actual newspaper contest where entrants ages 4 to 15 were asked to imitate "Deep Thoughts by Jack Handey."

"I believe you should live each day as if it is your last, which is why I don't have any clean laundry because, come on, who wants to wash clothes on the last day of their life?" --Age 15

"It sure would be nice if we got a day off for the president's birthday, like they do for the queen's. Of course, then we would have a lot of people voting for a candidate born on July 3 or December 26, just for the long weekends." -Age 8

"I bet living in a nudist colony takes all the fun out of Halloween." -Age 13

"For centuries, people thought the moon was made of green cheese. Then the astronauts found that the moon is really a big hard rock. That's what happens to cheese when you leave it out." -Age 6

"When I go to heaven, I want to see my grandpa again. But he better have lost the nose hair and the old-man smell." -Age 5

"If we could just get everyone to close their eyes and visualize world peace for an hour, imagine how serene and quiet it would be until the looting started." -Age 15

❖❖❖

Bizarre Celebrity Sex Scene Confessions

"His idea of a romantic kiss was to go "blaah" and gag me with his tongue. He only improved once he married Demi Moore. - Cybill Shepherd on Bruce Willis

"I enjoyed bumping up against it even though it had black stuff all over it...By the end of the shoot I was covered in black goo'." - Kim Bassinger being turned on by Michael Keaton's Batman costume.

Kenneth Williams's moment of unbridled passion with Joan Sims in *Carry On Up The Khyber* was somewhat marred by Williams's persistent flatulence.

Hygiene-conscious Lana Turner chewed gum to keep her mouth fresh for her kissing scenes. During the filming of *Homecoming*, Clark Gable kissed her so hard that the pair became entwined by a ribbon of sticky gum. From then on, she gargled.

"It's a little too sick, real or feigned to do in front of your mother." - Jennifer Jason Leigh stated about a sex scene in her 1996 movie, *Georgia*. Leigh asked her screenwriting mother, Barbara Turner, to leave the set at the crucial moment.

"God I miss my husband." - Patsy Kensit whispered to Mel Gibson during their naked romp in *Lethal Weapon 2*.

9

The Best of Readers' Comments

One of the biggest fears of any writer is that he or she will not be funny or clever enough. Fortunately, I do not have that worry because I have over six hundred thousand stringers in the form of Bizarre News readers. Every week, loyal "Bizarros" submit dozens of stories, lists and bizarre pictures, but the real wealth here is the comments I constantly receive. It's true that the readers' comments section of Bizarre News is just as well read as the stories themselves. So I know that if I happen to be off my stride one week, people will still enjoy their issue because of the comments. It was hard for me to select my favorites, since every issue has its gems, but I think the collection of comments in this chapter is and accurate representation of the wit and wisdom of Bizarre News readers (with my own come-backs frequently quoted afterward, of course). Enjoy!

I'm afraid I have to say that you are a truly ignorant, uncouth, unrefined, uncultured piece of Internet trash. What makes you think you have the right to call art "crap" simply because you do not understand it? I'm sure there are many things you do not understand, and if I were your wife I would try to get the hell away from you as fast as I could. People like you make me want to donate my entire pay to genetic science so that mistakes like you never happen again. Please remove me from your crappy, trailer-trash, Internet-rag-mailing list. I'm sure your audience of miscreants and mullet-men appreciate your low-brow satire, but I do not.

[See what happens when you let your mother-in-law subscribe?]

Lewis, this is one of the funniest things I've read for a while... "A 29-year-old man with both his legs in plaster and his arm in a sling died when he lost control of a car at high speed on the freeway near Newcastle. The driver had suffered two fractured legs and a broken collarbone in a car crash six days ago. Mr Geary, who could not wear a seat belt because of his injuries, was thrown from the car. He was dead when rescue services arrived at the scene. His wheelchair was found in the boot." - Ben Harlor

[You've got a morbid sense of humor, Ben.]

For a long time my husband was getting Bizarre News, editing it and passing it on to me. I thought he was AWESOME! Now that I know it's you finding all this great news I still think he's awsome, and I think you are TIGHT! My 14-year-old son says this is a good thing, but it sounds dirty to me. Thanks for making my week more fun. - Carol

[Thanks Carol. I think you're tight too.]

Lewis...I was listening to radio and heard about a man that LOVED to hide the TV remote from his wife and watch her look all over the house for it. Well, while she was looking she found a gun, and you guessed it...shot him to death. I know I won't hide the remote from MY wife.

[I do the same thing to my wife except with condoms.]

What exactly were you trying to say when you asked if we would want to be rich but brought up by Rosie and her lesbian wife? I was brought up by lesbian mothers and I turned out just fine. I am educated, have a good job, I am married (to someone of the opposite sex), and we are in the process of buying our first home. So what was your point? Because it sounded just a tad homophobic to me. - Misti

[I am NOT homophobic. By the way, can I have your mother's phone number?]

Dude, you're so ahead of the regular news it's scary. Jay Leno was talking about something last night that you already talked about a couple of weeks ago. Your journalistic abilities are pretty hard core!

[That's my motto: "Do it first, make it sensational, and the competition be damned."]

Here is something you may or may not have heard about. Take an old power cord and strip a bit of the insulation from the ends and wrap them around two nails. Poke them into the ends of a pickle and then plug in the cord. One half of the pickle will light up like a bulb. - Mike

[Thank you, Mr. Science, but I have a question; isn't "pickle" a slang term for a penis? You're not one of those freaky dungeon masters, are you?]

I'm sure you've heard of a rugby league player here in Australia called John Hopoate. He's just been banned for 12 weeks after sticking his finger up other players' backsides in an attempt to make them drop the ball. - Smitty in Sydney

[I bet he dropped it.]

I very much resent you alluding to all British having bad teeth. At least our children don't run rampant shooting everyone in school because the teacher or another student dared to criticize them or have half the population run around with guns in their pockets and fire first then think later.

[I heard that the "toothbrush" was invented in England. Anywhere else it would have been called "Teethbrush."]

I heard about a family that threw some glowing chicken bones in the dog's dish this morning. Apparently the FDA is looking into it. If that isn't a bizarre story waiting to happen, I don't know what is.

[I heard a story a while back about a young college kid who was bitten by a glowing spider....]

I read in a recent issue of *Cosmopolitan* magazine that some scientists are using MRIs to find new female g-spots. A couple had sex inside an MRI, and the woman told the researchers how she felt through a microphone while making love to her boyfriend. They then used the images to find out the angle of penetration etc, when she was feeling the most aroused and have actually identified a new g-spot already. Just thought you might like to know...

[Now that is an experiment I'd line up to participate in.]

Dear Lewis, One day my husband went fishing with me and the baby. Well, it was hot and no one was around. I stripped off my clothes and jumped in the water. I was downstream from where my husband was fishing when I felt something suckling my breasts. When I stood up, there were two large big mouth bass attached to my nipples. My husband yelled, "I must be using the wrong bait." - Jean B.

[The skeptic in me requires proof...please send photos.]

Lewis- I am a lesbian vampire, and Queeztal has yet to come get me. Any suggestions on what my girlfriend and I could do to get him down here to Idaho? Thanks, Andee

[I had forgotten about the hotbed of supernatural lesbian mysticism in Idaho.]

A sex-starved moose in Norway mistook a small, yellow car for a would-be partner, but defecated on it after it got no response. Leif Borgersen, owner of the Ford Ka model, said he found his car covered in lick marks, saliva and moose excrement.

[This must have been an Alabaman moose.]

Larry Causey figured he couldn't afford cancer treatment in a hospital, so he went to a place where it's free: jail. Causey, 57, called the FBI and told them he was about to rob the post office in West Monroe, Louisiana. At the post office, he handed a note to a teller demanding money, then left empty-handed and sat in his car until officers arrested him. "Larry's very sick, so getting arrested made him very happy," said Jay Nolen, Causey's lawyer.

[That's one way to get your tax money back out of the system.]

Hi, Lewis, I don't know if this qualifies as bizarre, but it shows that police in Georgia have nothing better to do. In DeKalb County an officer wrote a girl scout troup a ticket for peddling cookies outside a building without a license. I wonder if there is a badge for the girl scout first to be arrested. - Leisa

[Why should that be bizarre? Have you ever been accosted by one of those pint-sized entrepreneurs? That's high-pressure sales.]

Lewis, I came across this [high school's] website. I thought you would like it. You can see that the school's name and mascot is the "Butte Pirates". I hope you enjoy it. - Jason

[If I were the principal of Butte High School, I would not want the school mascot to be a pirate. But I'm not as progressive as some.]

How about [visiting] the Oklahoma Mr. Leather pageant? (This is a leather pageant for gay men). It's in Tulsa Oklahoma, and the owner of the pageant is a good friend of mine. If you wanted to go I could get you an interview with him.

[I thought there were only steers or queers in Tulsa and now you tell me there are both?]

Lewis, here's a little something I found at [*New Scientist* Magazine]... According to the Computer Fraud and Security Bulletin, a supermarket tabloid reports that two people were killed by a virus-infected computer in Valparaiso, Chile. The virus is said to have created a horned demon which decapitated one worker; the other died from a heart attack. The computer was exorcised.

[Alrighty. And people tell me I make up MY stories.]

Lewis you are just too good. I love your stories. I hope I can always get the Bizarre News. They are just too funny. Thanks for making my days worth it all. - Alice Rappold

[That's why we do it. Thanks for writing in.]

There is a town in Germany on the German/Dutch border called 'WANKUM'.

[In my adolescent days, geography was my favorite subject.]

I know Queetzal. I have met him. He used me, abused me, made me work as a phone sex operator, and ate my nachos.

[What part disturbed you the most? My money is on the nachos!]

You guys are absolutely fantastic. Please, please keep up the good work. I teach Modern Lit in a local University. I am telling all of my students to go to your site.

[Bizarre News should be required reading for all undergraduate students. I believe this is in the new Bush education plan.]

My brother used to work in a local hospital. While he was on duty one night, an ambulance came in with a man who had a small box wrench on his penis. He had been using it to masturbate but as his member became aroused he could no longer get the wrench off. They had to take him to surgery to cut it off. An awful lot of doctors came by to take pictures.

[And you wouldn't? You see, this is exactly why I only ever use an open-ended wrench to masturbate.]

Sun too close? We'll just change Earth's orbit. Fortunately, this article says that scientists have found a way to change the Earth's orbit by destroying a large asteroid around Pluto, blah blah blah...Some of the drawbacks: We may lose the moon [or] a miscalculation could hurl this asteroid into the Earth, leading to the death of all but microscopic life.

[Well, them's the breaks.]

Sure I masturbate at work every day. I can have an orgasm sitting in my chair, so why not? -Lisa

[So can I, but management frowns on it.]

Do you think the moon landing was a fake?

[There is supposedly a giant sound stage somewhere in the Nevada desert where the entire thing was filmed.]

Teachers at Pequot Lakes School in Minnesota are telling students to just say no to hugs. Hugging has become a standard greeting and way to say goodbye at Pequot Lakes. But the school isn't embracing the idea. Teachers are doling out reprimands to students caught hugging in the hallway. School officials think it's sexual and inappropriate.

[I completely agree. That's how is started at Columbine High School in Colorado. First hugging, then the semi-automatic weapons.]

I read this thing in the *Guardian* (big national newspaper here in the UK) that 80% of women admit to masturbating at work. Just thought you might be interested.

[I wonder if that's true here in the U.S. I'll have to start hanging out in the hall by the washrooms with a stethoscope. Any Bizarre readers care to share some stories?]

I find it rather scary that I now enjoy my time with you more stimulating than my time with my boyfriend. I think I may need therapy.-Shannan

[Not at all. Just subscribe your boyfriend to Bizarre News.]

Did you know that in Springs, Pennsylvania, men are legally forbidden to buy alcohol unless they have permission from their wives in writing?

[Please sell Juan some beer. Signed, Epstein's mother.]

You folks are just sick. Nothing in all my life comes close to the perversion you propagate upon the innocents of the world.

[That's our job. Bringing the weird to your mail box.]

I find that in moments of passion it's nice to say things like, "who's the serpent king?" Gets 'em every time.

[Well...who IS the Serpent King?]

I know you hear this a lot. But I get so tickled when Jay Leno or another entertainer tells a story that I read in your newsletter several days before. Ever wonder if they receive your newsletter and let you do all the work for them? - Emily

[Is that unscrupulous hack Leno using my material again?]

Dear Lewis: Thanks. I'm going to try giving MY dog St. John's Wort. - Nancy

[I had one of those removed with a laser a few years ago.]

Lewis, since you had the story about the Puerto Ricans who survived on breast milk, I wanted to tell you another story about the wonders of breast milk. I had a missionary friend who spent some time in India. One morning he opened the hood on his jeep and found a cobra piled on the engine. Before my friend could drop the hood, the cobra spat its poison in his eyes. Two villagers rushed over to him. The next thing my friend knew was he could feel a liquid that almost imediately stopped the pain. As he slowly regained his eyesight he saw the woman tucking her boob back into her top. The doctor later confirmed this by saying that breast milk actually neutralizes cobra poison and the woman saved his eyesight by acting so quickly.

[An important safety tip. Thanks, Egon.]

One of my favorite stupid laws is in Washington, which says you can be fined $500 for riding an ugly horse. P.S. Your publication kicks gecko balls! - Lisa

[That is at least one of the most ambiguous if not unique compliments I have ever received, Lisa.]

Lewis, I read in *Cosmopolitan* that an "average"-sized erect penis fits perfectly inside a toilet tissue roll. If you stick out you are longer than average, etc. I've told this to countless men, and not one has been able to resist taking the test. - Sheri

[I wonder if a paper towel roll would work?]

Lewis, are you ever going to reveal your secret identity to the world? I bet that people are wondering what you really look like!

[Alright. If you must know, I'm really Alan Greenspan.]

Lewis, did you hear the one about that lady in Los Angeles, California, weighing in at a whopping 450lbs? She thought she lost her wedding band down the sink forever only to find it in her belly button five years later!

[And the boundaries of good taste are once again pushed back even farther.]

Hey Lewis, I like the bizarre obituaries idea. I remember a story in San Diego about five years ago, about a woman who quit her job at the mortuary, just walked out in the middle of the day, and took a cab home. The cab got into an accident and she ended up back at the same mortuary in a couple of hours. Isn't THAT ironic?

[More like inevitable.]

I realized yesterday that reading Bizarre News is a lot like being wasted. You sort of go into this trance and laugh and laugh, get a little excited and tingly, then afterwards you can't remember a thing. Thank you, Lewis!

[I feel it prudent to caution my readers NOT to print out Bizarre News, shred it and then try to smoke it. Serious health risks may be associated with this action.]

Hello Lewis, I love your newsletter. Other anagrams for Bizarre News are: "Zanier brews", "Sewn brazier", "Brazier news", "Wren-size bra", "New zebra IRS" and "Z brews in ear". No, I didn't sit up all night figuring these out. I just ran it through my computer. Regards, Barbara

[Well, that's cheating.]

I've been subscribed for a short time, but I think you're WAAAAY better than Jerry Springer any day! You better not ever quit doing this or I'll sue you!

[Email newsletter publishers and the women who stalk them next on Jerry Springer.]

Lewis, I enjoy reading every aspect of your newsletter. From the Readers' Comments, I noticed that some of the readers are pretty anal retentive and a bit too politically correct. Do not let this influence you. I love to receive your newsletter in all its honesty and candor. Don't ever stop! - Staci

[It's true that email is the only way I have to keep my finger on the pulse of Bizarre News readers, but I do have my journalistic integrity, such as it is.]

I am not an art critique, but I have seen my fair share of art while in Paris and Madrid. There was a lot of beautiful work by many different people. Then I went to a "modern art" museum and saw what most people would call crap. This led me to the belief that everything is art, including belly button lint. - Adam

[Then you would love the guy I saw on television the other night who created "paintings" by vomiting on his canvas. I sat through a cock fight in an abandoned warehouse in Arizona, but I had to change the channel when this guy came on.]

51-year-old Maureen Shotton was subjected to a two-hour ordeal when she was imprisoned in a hi-tech public toilet. The toilet, which boasts state-of-the-art electronic auto-flush and door sensors, steadfastly refused to release Maureen and further resisted attempts by passers-by to force the door. She was finally liberated when the fire brigade ripped the roof off the cantankerous crapper.

[Sounds like the makings of a good science fiction movie.]

Your wife is a very lucky woman to be blessed with a man that has a sense of humor like yours. So, do you have a single brother?

[No, but I've got a pair of sisters.]

Lewis, thought you might like these 'unique' interpretations of the English language that I spotted on a recent holiday in Spain. These are taken from a Chinese restaurant menu in Bilbao: "Intriguing fibre source-Special bowel salad" and "Fuck Neck Sop."

[Would you believe me if I told you I've had Fuck Neck Sop?]

Lewis, this isn't as weird as the Angelina Jolie thing, but it is rumored that Billy Bob was caught at the gym wearing his wife's underwear. He said it makes him feel good because they don't get to see each other often. They were made for each other. - Krystal

[What's so bizarre about that? I'm wearing my wife's brassiere right now.]

I've heard people with genital piercings insist that they improved sex, but the first time I ever saw a guy with what is called a "Prince Albert" - a steel ring through the head of his penis, all I could think was, "Yeah... Like I'm gonna risk chipping a tooth on that." Just wanted to say that you're crazy, but I enjoy reading Bizarre News...keep up the good work. - John

[Thanks. I appreciate the comments!]

Lewis: First of all, I love your column. Secondly, I can appreciate your facination with UFOs. I had an encounter of the "second " kind as they say, in September 1972. I will never forget it and the marks that it left on the hood and top of my 67 volkswagon! They are curious to know about us. - Victoria in Texas

[A UFO attacked your '67 Volkswagen in Texas? Damned aliens.]

Lewis, I love this man! Please keep it coming. I haven't been on your news list long. However, I feel like I have come home. Thanks, Paul

[And I feel like I have had my refrigerator raided and my remote control commandeered.]

Lewis, you remain the William Randolph Hearst of the bizarre. Thank you for opening my eyes to things I much rather would have avoided. - Phil

[Thanks a lot. There is a famous quote from Hearst during the Spanish-American war (which it was rumored he started). An illustrator requested of Hearst that he be allowed to come home as everything in Havana was quiet. Hearst replied, "Please remain. You furnish the pictures and I'll furnish the war."]

Hello Lewis, I love your comments from your angry readers. It shows that your bizarre news is working!

[I feel that if at least a few dozen aren't shocked or offended than I haven't done my job.]

Lewis, I have to inform you that every issue of Bizarre News I get, I am ordered by my superior officers to bring it into work. Even though we have seen a lot of bizarre stuff in the Navy, it's good to hear we aren't the only ones with bizarre sea stories. Keep it coming, THAT'S an ORDER! - Chief

[Aye aye, Chief. Now can you answer a question for me...what is a swabby?]

Lewis, I think you're the greatest! You're charming, witty, smart and much funnier than TZ! Are you a real cutie, too? --Anita

[Is the duck-billed Platypus a monotreme?]

I had the pleasure of reading your newsletter today, and I haven't laughed so much in a very long time! I can't wait until tomorrow's reading!

[I don't see what's so funny about a bit of good investigative reporting. But as long as it keeps you informed and entertained, that's the most important thing.]

In Idaho we still have a law on the books that states that upon release from prison you are eligible for a good horse, $50 dollars or $50 dollars worth of gold, and a gun of your choice. - Bambi

[That's what I call faith in your rehabilitation system.]

Lewis, reading your column makes me tingle in my no-no area.

[Not to worry. Bizarre News is not sexually transmitted.]

Lewis, I just wanted to say keep up the great work. You rock like a parked van, man.

[Yes, I do.]

Lewis, I just had a bizarre thought. If we built a spaceship capable of traveling to another solar system, the trip would take several generations. A group of scientists would leave Earth, and after several generations of inbreeding, a bunch of Alabama'ns would step out on Alpha Centari.

[I think I saw an episode like that on Star Trek.]

Prostitutes in Cancun, Mexico, are going the way of soldiers, police and soccer players by donning uniforms for their work. About 50 prostitutes began using the uniforms - tight black shorts and yellow tops - while working Cancun's streets and bars in protest of a local council order that they move into a "zone of tolerance" outside the city center.

[All they need now is a price list.]

Lewis why is it that you always hear about men that have several wives, but not women having several husbands? Is this because women are smarter than men?

[Actually, paternity issues become difficult and men do not want to care for another man's child in most cases. Sociology class was my favorite!]

I just realized I've been subscribed to Bizarre News for over a year now. Wow! That'd explain a lot. You can scare and disgust people with it.

[And if you hit the print button on your computer, you never will need toilet paper again.]

Lewis, I once listened to this lecture given by an astronaut. He recalled how bubbles of water can float round in the cabin of the spaceship. He wondered, if you put a goldfish into the bubble of water, will it swim out? - Alyssa

[I'll put our science team on this one right away.]

Guess who the number one buyer of Bull Balls is? That's right, McDonald's. So you're not only getting your daily source of grease, you are also getting the protien. - Rebecca

[This information will save me a trip to Montana this year for the annual Testical Festival (which, by the way, occurs in September).]

Lewis, I thought you might want to look into something I heard in my World History class. Supposedly, in Japan you can buy hot dogs, condoms, and used women's panties from the vending machines. I'm not sure how true that is, but it would be interesting to find out! - Melissa

[And perhaps that's something we should adopt here in the U.S. Often while sitting in an airport or shopping somewhere I've thought to myself, "Golly, I could go for a hot dog and a pair of panties."]

A friend of mine was shot six times in the chest by her estranged husband. The only thing that saved her? Her breast implants.

[When did they switch from Silicone to Kevlar?]

Thank goodness for memories? Personally I say thank goodness for MAMMARIES! -Bill Blansfield

[Well, now 800,000 people know you're a sex fiend, Bill.]

A Finnish wildlife lover survived unscathed after a beaver tried to sink its teeth into his neck as he tracked it along a remote river. "I thought it would be nice to see the beaver jump into a river so I followed it. Suddenly the beaver disappeared and next thing I knew it was hanging on my neck."

[I bet this was the first time this guy was ever not happy to get a little beaver. Thanks to Shawna for sending this story.]

I just had to write and tell you about something I consider bizarre. Ever since we had the olympic games in Atlanta, our little town of Dublin, Georgia, has had the "redneck games". Events include bobbing for pigs feet, watermelon seed spitting contest, hubcap hurl, diving in a dumpster, and the big deal is the mud pit belly flop. What's sad is that last year it drew over 10,000 people! - Staci

[Interesting. I'm sorry to say that I could not realistically compete in any of those events. My talents are so limited in that respect. Anyway, I'm sure it makes for quite a bar-b-que.]

Lewis, is your sense of humor natural? - Keva

[No, actually. I had humor enhancement surgery done in '91.]

You did very well, Lewis! It was fun. Remember, men and your newsletters are like blenders. You need one, but you're not sure why. - Victoria

[I can clear that up for you. You need men because that lawn won't mow itself, and you need Bizarre News because the mainstream media is nothing but a liberal propaganda machine. At least that's what I've heard, anyway.]

While not as GROSS as bull semen, I had a bowlful of octopus eyes when I spent two months in Taiwan back in 1996. Actually, they were pretty good. Luckily, I was under the influence of Taiwan beer at the time. - Gerry White

[All those who think this is more gross than bull semen? The "Ayes" have it.]

Lewis, once when I was traveling through China I drank [snake] bile mixed with the local version of "white lightning". We had several rounds of "Gombe." The next thing I knew, I was signing Karaoke with three Chinese women. - Jim Rogers

[Everybody's got at least one "Gombe" story. Why is it that whenever you drink snake bile and grain alcohol you end up in a Chinese Karaoke bar?]

Hey Lewis, I hear that Jamie Lee Curtis is a hermaphrodite, is that true? I find it very hard to believe such nonsense but you just never know! - Jackie

[You know I'm not the kind of person to spread rumors, so I can neither confirm nor deny that Jamie Lee Curtis has a penis.]

Hi Lewis, I love your stuff. I used to buy *National Enquirer*, but I don't bother wasting my money now. I get all the entertainment free online from you. I laugh so much. I can never wait for your next email. - Wendy, Nottingham UK

[Thanks Wendy. I appreciate the support. I'm glad to know you're moved from that sensationalism on to a hard-line news periodical like Bizarre News. Stay tuned...next week we'll have more masturbation and breast enlargement stories.]

I went to visit a friend in Colorado. He told me I just had to try these "Rocky Mountain Critters." Well I tried 'em without knowing what they were - cow balls - yuck! - Erin Kelly

["Cow" balls? Erin, are you sure?]

Hi, Lewis! An even more bizarre item came to mind. Kopi Luak, an Indonesian coffee made from coffee beans retrieved from the feces of the Luak. The beans ferment in the digestive tract of this weasel-like creature, are collected from the feces, and processed. This coffee sells for up to $300 a pound to coffee connoisseurs.

[How often do you hear an Indonesian say, "This coffee tastes like $h!*?"]

Lewis, sometimes I just want to print out your newletter and cover myself with honey then stick your newsletter to me and run down the street. Would you put me in your newsletter if I get caught doing this?

[Yes, but you have to provide photos.]

Here's a story I thought you would find interesting. It seems some guy named G. Warren Shufelt, back in 1934 discovered a maze of tunnels underneath the city of Los Angeles. These tunnels were supposedly inhabited by a race of half-lizard, half-human beings.

[Nice effort, but I think this was an episode of "The Night Stalker."]

I love you, Lewis. You are all man. How I wish I could suck your toes. - Gabrielle

[And speaking of pushing boundaries.]

Hey, Lewis! I just working at a club in Detroit called "SPACE." It's a very unique club. We have little people, drag queens, a 300-pound dominatrix, flame jugglers, go go dancers and a few other things. I thought it might be worth checking out! Let me know, and I'll get you on the guest list. - Brian

[Have you been over to TZ's house, too?]

Hey Lewis, love your column! I saw in one the other day that it is illegal to kill or threaten a butterfly in California. Well, up here in Alaska it is a FELONY to kill a goose. I think they know this, too, because they are always walking across the busiest streets! - Deon Oliverson, Anchorage, Alaska

[Talk about having your goose cooked. Do you at least get to keep it if you hit one?]

I am in a band in San Diego and I always hate doing sound checks, until recently, I now take experts from your newsletters and read them before each show and I tell everyone to visit www.bizzarenews.com for more great stuff. - Chandra

[Thanks. If you ever need a front man let me know. I sing a mean "Proud Mary."]

Dearest Lewis...I was wondering how I could get in touch with Queetzal? I've been reading your newsletter for a long time now and I think that Queetzal is nearly as enigmatic and intriguing as you are, although he undoubtedly possesses slightly more sexual mystique than you (no offense Lewis, but that's the way things are). - Amanda Lynne

[I really don't know why, but I'm offended.]

Lewis, a friend of mine sent $29.95 for a penis enlargement product guaranteed to enlarge his penis by at least TWO to THREE times! After he received the package he was pissed off to find a friggin $1 MAGNIFYING glass!

[I guess that would do it.]

Lewis, I LOVE Bizarre. One of my favorite parts is the reader comments. I get a kick out of seeing whose buttons you've pushed this time. Just thought you should know that no matter what anyone says, my girls and I still love you. - Mandy and the FSU gang

[Please, God, let this be a sorority...]

Lewis, my favorite drinking toast is, "May the Bluebird of Paradise plant Mistletoe in your navel." - Dave

[Amen to that.]

Hey, Lewis! I've been reading your newsletter for over a year now, and I thank God every day that I'm not normal, so I can enjoy it! Thanks for the laughs. - Jenny S.

[Maybe you ARE normal and it's everybody else who's bizarre.]

Any chance on you dying soon so I can make some mad loot off your autographed book I won on eBay?

[I'll see that I can do for you.]

Lewis, would you dress up in a Batman costume and sneak in my bedroom? LMAO Your humor is awsome. - Rain

[No, sorry. But I do have a Captain America costume left over from a few Halloweens ago.]

Lewis, I love to read your newsletter every time is comes out. But I'm curious about a few things. First of all, who is Queetzal?

[That's a good question...who IS Queetzal?]

Tell me Lewis, do you and TZ really hang out outside of work?

[We've been hanging out more lately, since he figured out where my new house is.]

Lewis, in the interest of keeping my lunch down, I think I may have to find another time to read your newsletter!

[How about during foreplay?]

Hey, Lewis I just got a dog, a boxer! and I NAMED him LEWIS! Just like you!

[Thanks...I think.]

Hey Lewis - if you're the "bees knees" I've got some honey for you! - Anita

[Actually, I'm more like the bee's nephew.]

Mmmmm Lewis...I'm moving up your legs now. Toes were sweet. - Gabrielle.

[This is a note from my tailor. Don't forget to cuff the pants, Gabe.]

You are a funky, funky man Lewis. Kinda like funky monkey ice cream on a cold rainy July afternoon.

[I prefer mint chocolate chip if you must know.]

Lewis, you are about as twisted as they come, and I love you for it. Keep up the good work and snotty comments.

[I've been called many things, but rarely snotty. Well, I guess it's growth.]

Lewis, I've been subscribed to Bizarre News since way back before you guys took it over. I'm kinda torn about all these new subscribers. It's taking away that feeling of intimacy I used to have with you.

[I should have known not to let my proctologist subscribe.]

Once when I went to the DMV for my state ID I forgot to bring my birth certificate with me and they told me I didn't exist. - Jenni

[Maybe you don't. Do you ever get the feeling that everybody is ignoring you?]

Hey, Lewis, check out the latest of Entertainment magazine. "Doh", that famous quote of that oh-so-suave Homer Simpson, has now been added to the Oxford dictionary, so it's now technically a real word.

[There's only one thing I can say to that..."D'oh!"]

Hey Lewis, did you hear the story about the mother duck in British Columbia that grabbed a passing police officer by the pant leg and led him to a sewer grate where her baby ducklings had fallen in?

[Yes. A truly bizarre story. It seems the police removed the grate and helped out the ducklings, all the while the mother was there watching. And when they were rescued the mother calmly led them away. Thanks to everyone who sent this story to me.]

I just want to know one thing. What does it take to get a reader comment printed in Bizarre News? Do I need to send you a pair of panties or maybe some nude pictures of myself? - Chris

[Neither would hurt.]

I don't know if you covered this yet, but I saw a local news story showing an Austrailian town that gives its swim team a little extra incentive by releasing a saltwater crocodile into the pool behind them during practice. - Amanda

[And here I thought all Australian swimmers were fresh water.]

What exactly does the Oxford dictionary have as the definition for "d'oh"?

[A deer. A female deer.]

Why do women write in and offer to send you pictures of themselves in bikinis and naked and showing off their breasts?

[Because I'm sensitive.]

Alcohol and Calculus don't mix, so don't drink and derive.

[Cute.]

Lewis, I just wanted to let you know how much I love Bizarre News. Those people who keep sending you nasty comments just can't appreciate humor when they read it. As far as I'm concerned, you're cooler than a Chihuahua in a meat locker.

[Thanks.]

Lewis, did you hear about Claire Warburton who stunned traffic cops with her excuse for doing 105 mph when she told them "I haven't had sex for 48 hours and I'm desperate".

[Did the cops solve her desperation?]

Lewis, the world owes you a debt of gratitude. It's amazing how you can put such a humorous spin on how f'd up the world is. - James

[The world also owes me that 20 bucks I loaned it last week.]

Lewis, you rule like a yard stick! - Tony

[No reason to be boastful. 12 inches would be plenty for me.]

Guess what, Lewis! I'm no longer a danger to society!

[Why, have you unsubscribed to Laffaday?]